The Secrets Behind
High-Rise Condos

Chapter 0

プロローグ
Foreword

Chapter 0 プロローグ

東京湾岸地域を中心に、今日も100mを超える高さのタワーマンションが次から次へと、その巨大な姿を現しています。本書によって、これら「タワマン」と呼ばれているタワー型マンションについて、これまで明らかにされていなかった事業者、設計者、施工者、管理会社、そして住民の立場から、真の姿を知っていただきたいと思います。

もう少しタワーマンションのことを知りたいと考えている人、これからタワーマンションを購入したいと考えている人、今住んでいるがよくわからないことが多いと思っている人にこの本を読んでいただき、増え続けるタワーマンションとどのように付き合っていくかを考えるための一助になればと思います。

まず、タワーマンションには、地震は大丈夫か？ 避難はどうなるのか？ 火事はどうか？ 修繕はどうなっているのか？ 建替えはどうするのか？ 施工ミスがあった場合の対応は？ 通常のマンションと比べて桁外れの費用がかかるのでは？ など、様々な質問が多く寄せられます。反面、良好な立地と割安感のある価格で、飛ぶように売れているのが現状です。

現在、全国の分譲マンションの数は613万戸を超えています。昭和40年前半には数万戸に過ぎなかったものが、マンションブーム、マンション不況を繰り返しながらも、約50年間で100倍以上になっています。その中でタワーマンションは、平成9年の規制緩和以降、都心部を中心に次々と建設され、現在では1,500棟前後、住戸にして50万戸を超え、マンションの全体の約1割を占めています。

人口の減少で、2020年を境にマンション不況になることは様々な研究機関から指摘されている通りですが、タワーマンションだけは例外で、オリンピック後の選手村に大規模なものが計画されるなど、首都圏では今後も増え続けていくことは確実です。

本書で取り上げるタワーマンションとは、高さ60m以上で、共用廊下が建物の内側に配置されている、いわゆる内廊下タイプの建築で、1棟で住戸数が300戸を超える規模を想定しています。タワーマンションにはチェックすべき重要なポイントがいろいろあり、それらを詳しく知ってもらうため、本書の最後に「知っておきたい建設の知識」のセクションをもうけました。きっとタワーマンションのことが好きになり、そこでの生活も笑顔が溢れるものとなるはずです。

Foreword

Giant high-rise condominium buildings over 100 meter in height keep on popping up one after another these days most notably in the Tokyo Bay area. This book reveals the never-before-told naked truth about these high-rise condos from the viewpoints of developers, designers, maintenance companies and residents.

I prepared this book for people wanting to know more about high-rise condos, mulling the purchase, or already living in hi-rise condos and wanting to learn more in hopes of providing them with a better idea on dealing with high-rise condos.

About high-rise condos, people ask various questions on things like earthquake resistance, evacuation procedure, measures against fire, repair plan, rebuilding scheme, construction problem handling, overall costs against regular condos and so forth. At the same time, it's also true that high-rise condos sell very quickly with their attractive location and pricing.

Currently, we are seeing more than 6.1 million condo units in Japan. With repeated ups and downs in demands, the number grew more than 100 times in the last 50 years from a few tens of thousands units back in the late 1960s. As for high-rise condos, the deregulation in 1997 triggered the construction boom in central Tokyo, and now there are about 1,500 high-rise condo buildings with more than half a million units. This accounts for almost 10% of overall units.

Various research institutes predict a big setback in condo construction after 2020 with the shrinking Japanese population. However, high rise condos will not fall to the victim of this slowdown as there are many large-scale high rise condos in the planning including the one to be built at the athletes village site after the Olympics. We will surely continue to see more and more huge high-rise condos in the future.

In this book, high-rise condos are defined as the building with more than 60m in height, internal hallways and more that 300 units. As there are many things to look at concerning high-rise condos, I prepared the "Useful Information on Architecture" chapter at the end of this book. As you learn more about high-rise condos, you will like them even more and will enjoy your life there.

Chapter 0 ▍プロローグ

タワーマンションに関わる人々

建築の業界では、様々な呼び名が登場します。購入者、発注者、事業者などです（このように様々な名称があるのは、法律上の用語と一般的な呼称が混在しているからです）。たとえば、買主、売主は宅地建物取引業法の呼称です。中でも特に混同されやすいのが、建築士法上の監理者と建設業法上の監理技術者です。さらに、法規上と一般的な呼び方が混在し、各会社内での慣用的な「方言」も存在します。一般ユーザーの方々から見ると何が何だかわからないと思いますが、本書では分かりやすくするために、買主を購入者（竣工以後は区分所有者）、事業主、設計者、施工者（ゼネコン）、下請（サブコン）という名称を主に使います。

People Surrounding High-Rise Condos

You will encounter many people with different role names in this book such as buyer, contractee, contractor, and so on. To make things organized, we will use the notations listed on the opposite page. They have different names even for the same role as both legal and general names are used. For example, general notation of seller and buyer comes from the Act on Real Estate Transactions. This could be confusing, particularly many people get confused between managing supervisor of Act on Architects and Building Engineers and managing engineer of Construction Business Act because they sound similar in Japanese. Furthermore, in addition to the legal and general names mentioned above, each company has its idiomatic "dialects", and people would have a hard time understanding what is going on. In this book, we will be mainly using the following notations: buyer as purchaser (unit owner after completion), contractor, architect, constructor (general contractor) and subcontractor to minimize confusion.

Foreword

タワーマンションに係わる人々の呼称　People Surrounding High-Rise Condos

	購入者 Buyer	事業者 Developer	設計者 Designer	施工者（元請） Constructor	下請 （サブコン） Subcontractor
宅地建物取引業法 Act on Real Estate Transactions	買主 Buyer	売主 Seller			
建築士法 Act on Architects And Building Engineers		委託者 建築主 Contractee Client	建築士 監理者 Architect Administrator	工事施工者 Constructor	
建築業法 Construction Business Act		発注者 注文者 Owner Contractor		建設業者 元請負人 現場代理人 監理（主任）技術者 Constructor Main contractor On-site representative Chief engineer	下請負人 Subcontractor
一般名 General name	ユーザー オーナー 所有 User Owner	デベロッパー 事業主 Developer Contractor		ゼネコン 施工者 General contractor Constructor	協力会社 下請 サブコン Subcontractor

目　次

0 章 ▌プロローグ　　3
タワーマンションに関わる人々　　6

1 章 ▌タワーマンションの今　　15
マンションストック戸数　　16
表面利回り 5％　　18
建設業界の常識、非常識　　20
こうして生まれるタワーマンション　　22
収支最優先の現状　　24

2 章 ▌タワーマンションのデザイン　　27
デザインの基本　　28
設計者を見定める　　30
設計者も分業体制　　32
外観デザインのポイント　　34
色あせない内装デザイン　　36

3 章 ▌タワーマンションの基本構造　　39
骨格から決まるタワーマンション　　40
タワーマンションのコンクリートは最高級　　42
コンクリートの最大の弱点はひび割れ　　44
タワーマンションに求められる耐震性能　　46
耐震性の性能マトリクス　　48
耐震・制振・免震　　50
無被害の構造とは　　52
安全神話　　54
二段三段の備え　　56

4 章 ▌設計と施工　　59
設計品質　　60
設計監理と設計施工　　62
施工会社独自の工法や施工技術　　64
品質の本質は「ひと」　　66

5 章 ▌タワーマンションの内装　　69
仕様のグレード　　70
内装に見る事業者の覚悟　　72
床段差に見るタワーマンションの格　　74
たかが点検口、されど点検口　　76
クロスのグレード　　78

Table of Contents

Chapter 0 ∎ Foreword   3
People Surrounding High-Rise Condos   6

Chapter 1 ∎ High-Rise Condos Now   15
Number of Condo Units in Stock   16
5% of Gross Return of Profit   18
Common Sense and Lack Thereof in Construction Industry   21
How High-Rise Condos Are Created   22
Profit First   25

Chapter 2 ∎ Design of High-Rise Condos   27
Design Basics   28
Evaluating Architects   30
Task Sharing between Designers   32
Where to Look at in Exterior Design   34
Evergreen Interior Design   36

Chapter 3 ∎ Basic Structure of High-Rise Condos   39
Framework Shapes High-Rise Condos   40
Best-Quality Concrete Used in High-Rise Condos   42
Cracks, Weakest Point of Concrete   44
Earthquake Resistance Performance Required for High-Rise Condos   46
Performance Matrix of Earthquake Resistance   48
Seismic Resistance, Vibration Control and Seismic Isolation   50
Safest Structure in Past Earthquakes   52
Safety Myths   54
Multiple-Level Safety Measures   56

Chapter 4 ∎ Design and Construction   59
Design Quality   60
Design Administration Vs. Design and Construction   63
Construction Companies Developing Various Methods and Technologies   64
Essence of Quality-People   67

Chapter 5 ∎ Interior of High-Rise Condos   69
Specification Grades   71
Finding Contractor's Commitment in Interior   72
Judging Grade of High-Rise Condos from Entrance Floor   75
Access Panels-Peepholes to Quality   76
Grades of Wall Cloth   78

目 次

メーカーとの関係 … 80

6 章 ▍ タワーマンションの設備 … 83
最新設備が採用されているかどうか … 84
エネルギーを見極める … 86
天吊りカセット … 88
換気システムのグレード … 90
維持管理等級 3 とは？ … 92

7 章 ▍ タワーマンションの外構 … 95
植栽計画 … 96
桜は高級マンションの代名詞 … 98
風害対策のための街路樹 … 100
メンテナンスの重要性 … 102

8 章 ▍ タワーマンションの防災計画 … 105
地震時のタワーマンションの揺れの特徴と対策 … 106
地震時の避難の実態 … 108
避難安全検証法とは？ … 110
住戸内火災の避難のポイント … 112
タワーマンションでの避難方法 … 114

9 章 ▍ 購入者としての見極めポイント … 117
タワーマンションの魅力を演出する不動産会社 … 118
モデルルームは事業主のアピールの舞台 … 120
内覧会チェックポイント … 122

10 章 ▍ 維持管理の重要性 … 125
管理組合の役割 … 126
長期修繕計画の重要性 … 128
大規模マンションの修繕会計 … 130
タワーマンションの駐車場 … 132
ゴミ収集問題 … 134
LED 化の現状 … 136

11 章 ▍ 管理会社を見極める … 139
管理会社の姿勢 … 140
管理の質とは … 142
アフターフィードバックの重要性 … 144

12 章 ▍ 施工ミスはなぜおきる？ … 147
後を絶たない施工ミス … 148

Table of Contents

Relationship with Manufacturers	80

Chapter 6 ■ Appliances of High-Rise Condos — 83

Use of Latest Appliances	84
Examining Utilities	86
Ceiling-Mounted Air Conditioner Package	88
Grades of Ventilation System	90
Grade 3 of Maintenance Control Measures	92

Chapter 7 ■ Exterior of High-Rise Condos — 95

Planting Plan	96
Cherry Trees Represent High-Grade Condos	98
Street Trees to Prevent Wind Damage	100
Importance of Maintenance	102

Chapter 8 ■ Disaster Prevention Plan of High-Rise Condos — 105

Shaking Characteristics of High-Rise Condos in an Earthquake and Countermeasures	106
What Really Happened When an Earthquake Took Place	109
Verification Method for Evacuation Safety	110
Evacuating from Fire at Condo Unit	112
Evacuation in High-Rise Condos	114

Chapter 9 ■ Checkpoints for Purchase — 117

Realtors to Emphasize Charms of High-Rise Condos	119
Model Rooms – Developer's Theater	120
Checklist for Preliminary Inspection	123

Chapter 10 ■ Importance of Maintenance and Management — 125

Role of Owners' Maintenance Association	126
Importance of Long-Term Repair Plan	128
Repair Cost Accounting for Large Scale Condos	130
Parking Garage of High-Rise Condo	132
Garbage Collection Issues	135
On LED Lighting Deployment	137

Chapter 11 ■ Examining Maintenance Companies — 139

Attitudes of Maintenance Company	141
Quality of Maintenance	143
Importance of Post-Sales Feedback	144

Chapter 12 ■ What Causes Construction Mistakes — 147

Never Ceasing Construction Mistakes	148

目　次

品質向上を阻む建設業界の重層構造	150
IT化の弊害	152
杭設計の実態と課題	154

13 章 ■ タワーマンションの将来　157

地震国日本に根付きつつある超高層マンション	158
今、タワーマンションに求められるもの	160
空家問題	162
民泊問題	164
建設業界のIT化	166
これからのタワーマンションに求められるもの	168

14 章 ■ 知っておきたい建築の知識　171

新耐震設計法	172
長周期地震動	174
Is 値 0.6 の意味	176
地域係数 Z とは	178
日本の活断層	180
地盤の液状化現象	182
PML（Provable Maximum Loss）値とは？	184
見たことありますか？東京都耐震マーク	186
建築を取り巻く様々な法律	188
区分所有法	190
日本のリサイクル法	192
既存不適格建物とは	194
超高強度コンクリート	196
シートフローリング	198
ALC パネル	200
タワーマンションの工事工程の見方	202
大規模修繕工事の実際	204
サステナブル建築	206
超高層マンション改修ガイドライン	208
敷地の歴史をひもとく	210

Z 章 ■ エピローグ　213

Table of Contents

Construction Industry's Multi-Layered Hierarchy Blocking Quality Improvements	150
Issues Caused by IT Adoption	153
Facts and Issues of Pile Design	154

Chapter 13 ∎ Future of High-Rise Condos — 157

High-Rise Condos Becoming Common in Quake-Plagued Japan	159
What to Require Now in High-Rise Condos	160
Vacancy Problem	162
B&B (Bed and Breakfast) Issues	165
Promoting IT in Construction Industry	166
What to Require in Future High-Rise Condos	168

Chapter 14 ∎ Useful Information on Architecture — 171

Revised Seismic Design Method	172
Long-Period Earthquake Ground Motion	174
Meaning of Is Value 0.6	176
Seismic Zoning Coefficient Z	178
Active Faults in Japan	180
Soil Liquefaction	182
PML (Provable Maximum Loss) Value	184
Have You Seen the Tokyo Earthquake Resistance Sticker?	186
Various Acts Around Buildings	188
Building Unit Ownership Act	190
Recycling Regulations in Japan	193
Existing Non-Conforming Buildings	194
Ultra-High-Strength Concrete	196
Sheet Flooring	199
ALC (Autoclaved Lightweight Concrete) Panels	200
How to Read Construction Schedule of High-Rise Condos	202
Realities of Large-Scale Repair	204
Sustainable Architecture	206
Ultra-High-Rise Condos Renovation Guidelines	208
Studying Site History	210

Chapter Z ∎ Afterword — 213

Chapter 1

タワーマンションの今
High-Rise Condos Now

Chapter 1 ▍タワーマンションの今

マンションストック戸数

右の図が、国土交通省が毎年集計しているマンションストック戸数のグラフです。いわゆるマンションブームというものは第5次まであありますが、日本列島改造論やバブル景気など、経済情勢や政策によって引き起こされていることがわかります。とりわけ平成9年の規制緩和により、それまで郊外や河川周辺に建設されていた大規模マンションが、都心部、特に湾岸地域で建設されるようになり、東京湾岸地域の風景を一変させることになりました。なかでも汐留旧国鉄貨物駅跡地に建設された東京ツインパークスは、大手不動産三社(三菱地所、三井不動産、住友不動産)を中心とした不動産業界初の都心型タワーマンションとして建設され、その後のタワーマンションの計画に大きな影響を与えていくこととなります。同時期、佃島や芝浦地域の開発なども進み、一棟で1,000戸を超える巨大タワーマンションが現れます。その後、「姉歯事件」※1後のマンション不況を経て、タワーマンションは投資対象としての価値が高まり、今後平成9年の規制緩和以降、最大となる戸数の供給が見込まれています。

※1 一級建築士の姉歯秀次氏が、100件近くの建物で構造計算を捏造して耐震性に問題がないように見せかけていたことが2005年に発覚し、一部のホテルは解体され、多くのマンションの住人が退去を余儀なくされた事件

Number of Condo Units in Stock

The figure on the right page shows the number of condo units in stock reported in the annual report from the Ministry of Land, Infrastructure, Transport and Tourism. We have gone through five so called condo booms thus far, all triggered by economic situations and government policies such as Kakuei Tanaka's "Plan for Remodeling the Japanese Archipelago" and several bubble booms. Among those, the deregulation of the City Planning Act in 1997 started moving the condo construction from suburbs and riversides to central Tokyo, in particular the bay area,

High-Rise Condos Now

and that completely changed the scenery of the area. Most notably, the Tokyo Twin Parks built as the first high-rise condo in central Tokyo at the former Shiodome Freight Terminal site by the big three of the real estate industry, Mitsubishi Estate, Mitsui Fudosan and Sumitomo Realty & Development with help from other companies made the big impact on the high-rise condo building plans thereafter. Around that time, the construction development in Tsukudajima and the Shibaura area made progress and giant high-rise condos with over 1,000 units per building started to appear. Then after going through the downturn caused by the "Aneha Incident"[※1] in 2005, we are now expecting the biggest supply of condo units since the deregulation in 1997.

※1 Architect Hidetsugu Aneha falsified the structural calculations on building plans for about 100 buildings to make them look earthquake safe. Several hotels had to close for razing and many families were forced to vacate their relatively new condominiums.

全国のマンション数変遷 Increasing Number of Condo Units

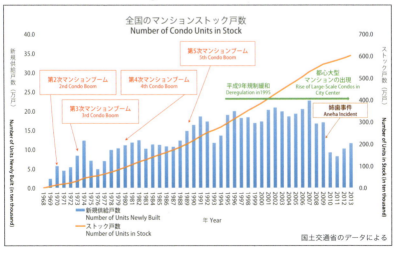

The Secrets Behind High-Rise Condos ∎ 017

Chapter 1 ┃ タワーマンションの今

表面利回り5%

それでは、増え続けるタワーマンションをどのようにとらえるか。本書の主題でもありますが、まず不動産業界、設計業界、建設業界と様々な角度から検証し、その実態を明らかにしていきたいと思います。

冒頭から業界用語ですが、不動産業界では「表面利回り」という言葉を使います。5,000万円のマンションを年間家賃250万円で貸したとき、家賃の価格に対する割合は250/5000＝0.05となり、これを表面利回り5％という呼び方をします。オフィスビルでよくいわれるのは、オフィスビルの建物の価値が賃料収入で決まるということです。タワーマンションも今や投資対象として同様な評価がされており、特に駅近（徒歩5分程度）のタワーマンションでは、この5％が一つの目安となります。一年に300万円の家賃が入るマンションでは、価格として6,000万円が価値判断の目安になります。これ以上だと割高、これ以下だと割安という感覚です。住宅ローンなど返済能力から買える価格を想定して、購入住戸を決めるという方法もありますが、鉄筋コンクリート造の減価償却期間は47年（固定資産税を算出する根拠となる建物評価額が47年で0となります）と定められています。100年、200年と資産価値を維持するためには、賃料からマンションの価値を見ておくことも必要です。

5% of Gross Return of Profit

Now, let's dive into the subject of the book, ever-increasing high-rise condos and examine them from various perspectives of real-estate, architecture and construction industries.

Sorry about the abrupt use of an industrial jargon, but we often use the term "gross return of profit" in the real-estate industry. When you lease a condo priced at fifty million yen for 2.5 million yen a year, the gross return of profit becomes 5% (i.e., 2.5 million divided by 50 million).

High-Rise Condos Now

The value of the office building is often determined by the rent income. Now that high-rise condos are the target of investments, this applies to them as well. This 5 % number is considered to be the measure for the high-rise condos located within a 5-minute walking distance from the nearest train station. Let's calculate the condo price back from the rent. The unit collecting 3 million yen rent per year is considered to be worth 60 million yen. If the price tag is lower than this, you could say it's cost effective, and vice versa.

You can decide what you can afford from the mortgage loan and your solvency. There, keep in mind that reinforced concrete buildings are completely depreciated in 47 years in Japan (meaning the assessed value of the building becomes zero after 47 years) and it would be necessary to observe the value of the condo from this rent point of view in order to maintain the property's asset value for the next 100 or even 200 years.

2020年過去最大の供給が見込まれている超高層マンション
Largest Supply of High-Rise Condos Expected in 2020

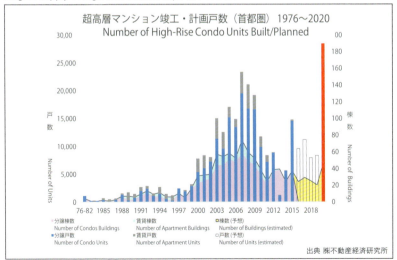

Chapter 1　タワーマンションの今

建設業界の常識、非常識

ほとんどの人にとって、マンションは一生でも最大級の買い物ですから、納得のいくまで十分検討することが重要です。たとえば、建築関係の知人の紹介で買ったのに、住んで1ヶ月もたたないうちにお湯が出なくなったり、最上階の屋根からの雨漏り跡が天井についたり、アフターサービスの窓口の対応も遅々として進まない。文句を言おうにも誰にいったら良いのかわからない。こんな状況でも知人は、「住宅はクレーム産業」と平気な顔で言ったり、一体どこに問題があったのか見当もつかなくなりますが、家族はしっかりと根を下ろし始めます。知人の紹介で買ったのにという思いが心に引っかかりつつ日々が過ぎていく、そんな思いをする人も少なくありません。きれいに飾り付けられたモデルルームやオプションの数々。事業者が売るためにつくったその中で、マンションの真の姿を見ることはなかなか難しいものです。これは業界の常識と購入者の認識にズレがあることから生じます。その例としてまず挙げられるのが、耐震性についての認識です。「耐震は基準法の最低限で十分」という考えが業界内にはあります。低層建物であれば、都心の一等地の10億ションも郊外の2,000万円代のマンションも、耐震性は同じというのが業界の常識です。日本の耐震工学は世界でもトップクラスではありますが、そのことがあたかも地震に対して安全であるかのような一種の錯覚を引き起こしています。実際は上記のような考えから、必ずしも耐震性を高くしているとは限りません。これは、高い耐震性を売りにしても、販売促進につながりにくいということが背景にあるからです。そもそも耐震性の説明自体営業的に難しく、「基準法」という説明ですませてしまいがちです。また、昭和56年以降の新耐震設計で設計された建物が、その後の大地震の際、それ以前の建物と比べ、被害が格段に減っているということも上記の錯覚の一因です。最近では免震構造も普及してきていますが、マンションではまだまだこれからという感じです。また、耐震設計を購入者に説明する際、住宅性能評価制度の中で規定されているレベルが使用されていますが、建物強度や地震強度との関係がどの程度理解されているか疑問です。今、世界中でマグニチュード9クラスの巨大地震が頻発しています。建築の耐震性を根本から見直す時期にきているのではないかと感じています。

High-Rise Condos Now

Common Sense and Lack Thereof in Construction Industry

As buying a condo in general is the most expensive shopping experience, you should look at every detail very thoroughly until you feel completely comfortable.

Still, hot water could stop working within a month after you move in, then the leak from the top roof could stain your ceiling in your condo and you don't know who to complain to. Also, the service response could be painfully slow. In the meantime, your family is getting adjusted to the new environment and days go by, but you still have a sour feeling about the support. But when you come to think about the fact that the model homes are beautifully decorated with numerous options for sales purposes, it would be very difficult to see the true state of the condo units. This is caused by the perception gaps between sellers and buyers, and the most obvious one lies in the earthquake resistance.

Many people in the construction industry say the lowest level of earthquake resistance stated in the Building Standards Act would suffice. It is well known in the industry that the earthquake resistance level of billion-yen condos in the city center would not be any different from that of twenty-million-yen-class condos in suburbs as long as they are low-rise building. The fact that Japan is one of the leaders of seismic engineering causes an illusion that the buildings in Japan are earthquake proof. In reality, the higher level of earthquake resistance will not help promote the sales of the condos. Also, explanation of earthquake resistance is a difficult task for sales people to start with, and conformance to the Building Standards Act would easily make more sense to ordinary people. Also, there's very little damage in the buildings conforming to the earthquake resistant design standards after 1981. Base isolation structure is getting popular, but it might take a while to become the mainstream. Levels 1, 2 and 3 defined in the Residential Performance Evaluation System are referred to during the explanation of the earthquake resistance design to buyers, but it's highly questionable whether they get the accurate picture of the resistance of building and its relationship with the earthquake intensity.

Now that magnitude 9 class earthquakes are taking place all over the world, it seems it's about time we need to reevaluate the earthquake resistance of buildings from scratch.

Chapter 1 ▌ タワーマンションの今

こうして生まれるタワーマンション

現在、タワーマンションの事業主、発注者としての大手不動産会社には、三井不動産、三菱地所、住友不動産、野村不動産などの4社があります。これらの不動産会社にとって最も重要なのは用地を取得し、事業収支を予測して応札価格を決めることです。そのために、これまでの実績や経験、人脈を駆使し、用地取得にこぎつけます。まず一般的には、コンピュータへの簡単な入力で、過去の様々なデータを元に事業収支計算をします。たとえば、土地取得額100億円、建設費200億円、一戸当たり施工費用 3,000万円、粗利10% といった具合です。一方で、土地の購入会社が入札などで決まった場合、業界新聞に計画内容が発表されます。用地取得段階からゼネコンが関わっている場合もありますが、早速メーカーなどからの営業攻勢がかかります。設計事務所が用地取得に関わることがありますが、そうなるとまさに総動員態勢です。ゼネコンは設計を手がけ設計施工とすることで自社仕様が採用しやすくなり、コストダウンの余地が広がり、利益へとつながっていきます。事業者も、ゼネコンの独自工法を使うことで一段とコストダウンができることもあり、大手設計事務所が参画する場合以外は、ゼネコンの設計施工となることが多くなります。一方で設計事務所が参画する場合、設計事務所とゼネコンの力関係から事業推進体制が決まります。

購入者から見た場合、設計監理者がゼネコンと同じ社内であるというのは、十分なチェック体制がとれるかどうか疑問が残ります。設計者が単なる図面作成者になっているのではないかといわれる理由です。

How High-Rise Condos Are Created

Currently, there are four major real estate companies in Japan noted as the high-rise condo builders and contractees. They are Mitsui Fudosan, Mitsubishi Estate, Sumitomo Realty & Development, and Nomura Real Estate Development. Most important tasks for these company are to obtain a piece of land, to estimate the business balance, and to set the bid price. They fully utilize their track record, past experience and connections to obtain the land. And then their software built on their various past data takes rather simple inputs, estimates the business balance, and outputs numbers such as 10 billion yen for land acquisition, 20 billion for overall construction and 30 million per unit, and 10% of gross profit. When the land purchaser is decided by bidding, the plan will be announced in industrial newspapers. Unless certain general contractors are already involved from the land purchase phase, intensive sales activities from equipment manufacturers will begin. This can be called "total mobilization" as even design offices may get involved in land acquisition. General contractors prefer design and construction approach so that they can use their specification for further cost reduction that ultimately generates increased profit. By using general contractor's own technologies, developer will benefit from further cost reduction, and this is why general contractor usually takes the design and construction approach unless some major design office is involved. When a design office is involved, their relationship of power with the general contractor will define the business promotion system.

On the other hand, from buyer's point of view, you might wonder if there would be sufficient checking mechanism in place when designer and administrator belong to the same company. This is why some people say architects are just drawers these days.

タワーマンションの企画から引き渡しまで High-Rise Condos - From Planning to Handover

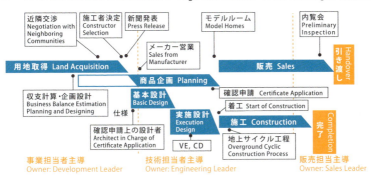

Chapter 1　タワーマンションの今

収支最優先の現状

事業者では、一般的に商品企画に販売の意見が反映されます。企画段階で概略の最大戸数や各住戸面積を想定し、これまでのデータや広告代理店を通じてのリサーチ結果などとともに総合的に判断して計画が進められていきます。

プラン全体は事業者主導によって決定されることが多く、設計者は、外観、共用部の設計、避難計画や防災計画などを進めることになります。基本設計段階から実施設計段階になると、事業各社の仕様に対しての採用の可否、そのコストの算出が主な作業となり、着工予定日時までに確認済証を受け取ることが至上命題となります。

着工までに建設費が予算内に収まらない場合は、着工後に VE (Value Engineering)[2]やCD (コストダウン) を行うこともあります。

収支を最優先する事業者には高い収益性、施工者にとっては技術力を生かした収益性、購入者もこれまでにない住環境を手に入れられるというように、三者それぞれに魅力があることが、今のタワーマンション人気を支えているといっても過言ではないでしょう。

---

[2] 製品の品質や信頼性を損なわずにコストの低減を図ること

High-Rise Condos Now

Profit First

Opinions from sales will be most valued when finalizing the marketing plan of the condos. Together with the ballpark figures of the number of units and their floor space they decided in the planning phase, they go ahead with the plan by combining the data from previous projects with the marketing research results from ad agencies and proceed on planning.

Overall planning is usually led by the developer, and the architect will proceed on designing the exterior and the common area, and on disaster prevention plan including evacuation. When the design phase progresses from basic design to working drawing, the main task will change to decision making on which manufacturer's specifications to use followed by the cost calculation. The ultimate goal at this point is to obtain the certificate of verification without delaying the construction schedule.

Sometimes they may start construction without containing the cost within the budget with possible value engineering[2] and further cost reduction during the construction in mind.

High-rise condos are very attractive to all sellers, contractors and buyers with their high profitability taking advantage of contractor's high-quality engineering, along with the superior living environment. These are the driving force behind the popularity of high-rise condos.

---

[2] A method to reduce the cost without sacrificing the quality and the reliability of the product

Chapter 2

タワーマンションのデザイン
Design of High-Rise Condos

Chapter 2　タワーマンションのデザイン

デザインの基本

ひときわ目を引くタワーマンションは、都市の風景を一変させます。その特徴は、ダイナミックな空間構成と広い敷地を生かした外構計画にあります。

タワーマンションの外観のデザインは、建物の高さ、階高やスパン、骨組の構成、断面計画により必然的に決まります。具体的には、ファサードの連続性、階高とスパンのプロポーションなど、構造から決められた条件の下でのデザインとなりますが、さらに建物全体のプロポーションや周辺環境との調和といった様々な要素が含まれます。また、東京都中央区佃島のタワーマンション群のように、橋や川といった周辺環境を取り込んで美しい都市景観を形づくっている地域があります。浜離宮からの汐留地区の景観には、東京ツインパークスが欠かせない存在となっているように、今やタワーマンションは、都市景観を形づくる上で不可欠な要素となっています。その意味でも、東京湾岸地域のタワーマンションの設計者には、レム・コールハース著の「錯乱のニューヨーク」に是非目を通してほしいものです。

Design Basics

Extremely eye-catching high-rise condos will change the urban landscape substantially. They are very different from other buildings with their dynamic space utilization and beautiful exterior plan taking advantage of their extensive premises. Exterior design of high-rise condos is determined by building height, floor height and span, framework configuration and cross section plan. Also, the design will be constrained by structure such as structural continuity and proportion between floor height and span. In reality, there are various other factors like overall building proportion, balance with surrounding environment and so on. Some high-rise condos, for example the ones in the Tsukudajima area of Tokyo's Chuo-ku, form a gorgeous view by blending in perfectly with their surroundings such as bridges and rivers. Nowadays, high-rise condos are the essential element of the city landscape.

Design of High-Rise Condos

The view of the Shiodome area from the Hama-Rikyu Gardens would be totally lackluster without the Tokyo Twin Parks.
In that sense, Rem Koolhaas' "Delirious New York" is a must read for the architects of the high-rise condos in the Tokyo Bay area.

東京都中央区佃島 (Tsukudajima area of Tokyo's Chuo-ku)

東京都港区汐留地区 (Shiodome area of Tokyo's Chuo-ku)

Chapter 2 タワーマンションのデザイン

設計者を見定める

タワーマンションの外観デザインの特徴は、建物の表裏がないことでメインエントランスの他にサブエントランスがいくつか設けられます。このサブエントランス廻り、特に通用口や車路のデザインに、事業者や設計者の気遣いがみてとれるタワーマンションは、一段上のレベルと言って良いでしょう。

一例ですが、スペインのバルセロナにある建築家アントニオ・ガウディ（1852～1926）の設計した世界遺産のカサ・ミラ、カサ・バトリョ等は、建物裏側のフェンスに至るまで見事にデザインされており、目に見えるものは排気塔まですべて独自の形状となっています。

タワーマンションに限ったことではありませんが、人の目につかないところへの気配りに、事業者、設計者の質を垣間見ることができます。

Evaluating Architects

One of the distinctive features of high-rise condo buildings is the fact that they have no front or back side, and therefore, they are equipped with several sub-entrances in addition to the main one. And if you see some craftsmanship of the architect or the contractor there, you are definitely looking at the higher-grade condo building.

For example, at Casa Milà and Casa Batlló, World Heritage sites in Barcelona, Spain, both designed by Antonio Gaudi (1852 -1926), everything you could see including back fences and ventilation shafts is uniquely and beautifully designed. You can catch a glimpse of the qualities of the architects and the contractors in the minor detail of the hidden corners of the building.

Design of High-Rise Condos

バルセロナのガウディ設計による建造物　Works by Gaudi in Barcelona

サグラダ・ファミリア　Sagrada Família

カサ・ミラ　Casa Milà

カサ・バトリョ　Casa Batlló

Chapter 2　タワーマンションのデザイン

設計者も分業体制

タワーマンションでは、建物全体の設計者の他に、有名なデザイナーを外装デザインや内装デザインに起用することがあります。中には海外の著名なデザイナーを起用して、販売戦略のための話題づくりをすることもあります。このとき、デザイナーが共用部の内装を担当している場合は、カーテン、備品、照明に至るまで世界中からとりよせた様々な素材をアレンジし、独自性の高いものとなっていることが多いのですが、改修の際にそのデザインコンセプトや設計者の叡智の集積をいかに継承できるかという課題が残ります。多くのデザイナーの個性がぶつかり合う中で、全体としてのまとまりをどのように演出するか、事業者の力量が問われます。外観とメインエントランス、インテリアなどにデザインの違和感があるとすれば、事業者の中途半端なコンセプトづくりが原因であったといえるでしょう。

Task Sharing between Designers

In addition to the chief architect, contractors sometimes hire famous designers for exterior and interior design. They even bring in some big names from overseas to make a big splash. When an overseas designer is in charge of the interior design of the common areas, he/she tends to gather and arrange various interior objects from curtains, furnishings to lightings from all over the world to create a highly unique atmosphere. On the other hand, it would be a challenging task to inherit such a collective integration of design concepts and know-hows of these designers when a repair becomes necessary. It is up to the contractor's skill whether they can create the sense of overall harmony from different designers' often diverging originality. If you feel some design discrepancy between the exterior, the main entrance and the interior, it is highly likely the contractor did not have a clear concept at the beginning.

Design of High-Rise Condos

建築設計の分業体制 Design Task Sharing of Architectural Work

Chapter 2 | タワーマンションのデザイン

外観デザインのポイント

外観デザイン上のポイントの一つに、コーナー部の形状があります。最もシンプルな全周バルコニー方式から、オフィスビルに近いバルコニーがほとんどないものまで多種多様な形状があります。眺望の良さからR形状のものが人気プランですが、日射による冷房負荷や室内の家具のレイアウトなどを考える必要があります。

建物最上部のデザインは設計者にとっての見せ場です。下からの伸びやかな連続性の延長上でいかに空につながり、周辺環境と調和しつつ存在感を示せるかが都市の象徴的景観の一つとなっているからです。

Where to Look at in Exterior Design

One of the design highlights of high-rise condos is the corner of the building. There are many options from the simplest choice of surrounding balcony to nearly no balcony as with office buildings. Round shape is most popular from the view standpoint, however, you need to take things like air conditioning burden caused by sunshine along with furniture layout into account.

Also, the topmost design would be where designers can show off their skills. It is up to him/her how to smoothly stretch the building shape from the bottom up to the sky. High-rise rooftops have definitely become one of the representative cityscapes.

Design of High-Rise Condos

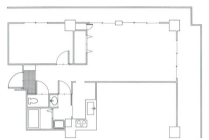

全周型バルコニー Surrounding Balcony

バルコニーなし No Balcony

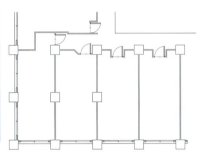

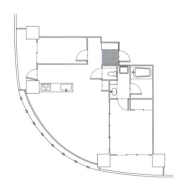

R型バルコニー Round-Shaped Balcony

The Secrets Behind High-Rise Condos ▍ 035

Chapter 2 タワーマンションのデザイン

色あせない内装デザイン

タワーマンションの耐用年数を考えるときに、他に真似のできない色あせない内装デザインがなされているかは大きなポイントです。その一例として、池袋にあるアメリカの建築家フランク・ロイド・ライトの設計による重要文化財・自由学園明日館(1921年、大正10年築)という現存する建物が挙げられます。今も地域の様々な活動に利用されており、決して華美ではないものの、池袋の喧騒と裏腹にここには穏やかな時間が流れています。「簡素な外形のなかにすぐれた思いを充たしめたい」という当時の建築主、羽仁吉一・もと子夫妻の思いと、それに応えた建築家の姿勢が、94年たった今もなお息づいています。タワーマンションに求められるデザインには、このようなものが必要ではないかと思います。余談ですが、フランク・ロイド・ライトの自邸も、100年以上たった今でもシカゴ郊外に静かにたたずんでいます。

Evergreen Interior Design

Considering the long lifespan of high-rise condos, it would be important to have very original and evergreen interior design. As a good example of such design, one of Japan's important cultural assets, Jiyu Gakuen School's Myonichikan building (built in 1921) located in Toshima-ku of Tokyo designed by American architect Frank Lloyd Wright comes to my mind. The building is still well in use for many various local activities. The design is far from being gorgeous, but it manages to maintain a sense of tranquility against its rather noisy surroundings of the busy Ikebukuro area. After 94 years, you can still feel the intent of the clients, Yoshikazu and Motoko Hani and the architect's response to fill excellent ideas into a simple exterior form, and this is what we need for the interior design of high-rise condo buildings. Just an aside, Frank Lloyd Wright's own home in suburban Chicago stands quietly still after more than 100 years since it was built.

Design of High-Rise Condos

重要文化財　自由学園明日館
設計フランク・ロイド・ライト (1921)
Jiyu Gakuen School's Myonichikan
building by Frank Lloyd Wright (1921)

フランク・ロイド・ライト自邸 (シカゴ郊外)
Frank Lloyd Wright Residence (Suburban Chicago)

Chapter 3

タワーマンションの基本構造
Basic Structure of High-Rise Condos

Chapter 3 タワーマンションの基本構造

骨格から決まるタワーマンション

建築物を設計する際にはまず建築基準法（188ページの「建築を取り巻く様々な法律」を参照）を満たすことが求められますが、タワーマンションの場合、通常のマンションと大きく異なるのが、外観ではなく建物の骨格から決まる点です。

建物規模から必然的に柱の大きさ、スパン等が決まり、それらを可能にするコンクリートの強さや鉄筋の強さが決まります。

特に柱の大きさは、空間の有効率や外観のデザインを左右することから、いかに強く細くするかが重要で、ここに施工者の技術力が問われます。

Framework Shapes High-Rise Condos

Architectural design requires conformance with the Building Standards Act (see "Various Acts Around Buildings" on page 188). Unlike other condos, the building framework will be the determining factor in the case of high-rise condos and not the exterior appearance.

The size of the building determines the size of the columns and the span between them, and consequently the strength of the concrete and the reinforced rods to support them.

As the size of the columns in particular has a big impact on the space efficiency rate and the exterior design, it would be extremely important to make it as strong and as thin as possible, and this is where the technical capability of the constructor really shows.

Basic Structure of High-Rise Condos

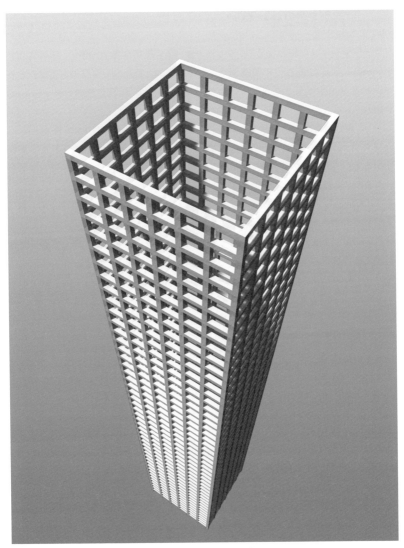

タワーマンションの骨格　Framework of High-Rise Condo

Chapter 3 タワーマンションの基本構造

タワーマンションのコンクリートは最高級

タワーマンションに使われるコンクリートは、最低耐用年数100年の、高強度コンクリートと呼ばれるもので製造プラントも限られ、普通コンクリートとは異なり一段高度な品質管理がなされています（196ページの「超高強度コンクリート」を参照）。

しかし、高強度ならではの課題もあります。設計基準強度 80N/mm² を超えると、コンクリート内に残された表面付近のわずかな気泡が火災の際に爆裂する可能性があるのです。この危険性は、ポリプロピレンを細かくしたチップを混入するという方法で防止することができます。

高さ100m前後のタワーマンションで、1階の柱の強度を70N/mm² 前後とし、ポリプロピレン混入によるコスト増を回避するために、あえて断面を大きくしている場合があります。それによって住戸の有効面積が減りますので、購入の際には平面図で柱の位置と大きさを確認するようしたいものです。

最近、100年コンクリートを謳ったものがありますが、セメントや水の量などあくまでもコンクリート仕様のことで、必ず100年もつわけではありません。詳細は日本建築学会の「建築標準仕様書・同解説 JASS 5 鉄筋コンクリート工事2015」をご参照ください。

Best-Quality Concrete Used in High-Rise Condos

The concrete used in high-rise condos is called high strength concrete with minimum 100-year durability and is manufactured in selected plants with stricter quality control than usual (see "Ultra-High-Strength Concrete" on page 196).

However, the high strength concrete has its own problem. When the strength exceeds 80 N/mm², small number of bubbles close to the surface may cause explosive fractures in the case of fire. The known solution to this is to Inject small chips of polypropylene into concrete.

Basic Structure of High-Rise Condos

Some constructors use columns with larger cross section but with lower strength around 70 N/mm² in high-rise condos of about 100 m of height in order to avoid the cost increase by this polypropylene injection. You need to pay attention to this when buying a condo as the unit area will decrease in such a case.

Some developers claim the use of 100-year concrete these days, but they are just talking about the specs of the concrete such as the ratio of the water content in the concrete, and therefore, there's no guarantee for actual 100 year endurance. Please refer to Japanese Architectural Standard Specification for Reinforced Concrete Work JASS5 (2015) published by Architectural Institute of Japan for detail.

コンクリート試験 Concrete Tests

流動性の高い高強度コンクリート
Highly Fluid High-Strength Concrete

爆裂防止用ポリプロピレンチップ
Polypropylene Chips to Prevent Explosive Fractures

Chapter 3 タワーマンションの基本構造

コンクリートの最大の弱点はひび割れ

タワーマンションに使われる高強度コンクリートは、一般のコンクリートより含まれる水の量が少ない分、密度も高く乾燥収縮によるひび割れが発生しにくくなっています。また、工場内で品質管理されているため、仕上がり状態も高いレベルといえます。しかし、弱点もあります。震度5程度でも、梁の端部に0.1mm程度のひび割れが入ってしまうことです。0.3mm程度まではコンクリートの劣化に影響はないとされていますが、地震によるひび割れは、一度開いて閉じている貫通ひび割れです。台風など横からの風雨にさらされるコーナー部の窓の部分は、サッシが直に梁に取り付けられているため、漏水の可能性もあり、外壁点検の重要項目としておくことが必要です。

Cracks, Weakest Point of Concrete

High strength concrete used for high-rise condos contains less water, and therefore, is denser and more resistant to drying shrinkage cracking. Also, strictly controlled manufacturing process gives better finishing. Unfortunately, there's also a drawback. It will create small cracks of about 0.1mm width even with a seismic intensity of 5 at ends of beams. Even though cracks less than 0.3mm wide are considered to be no threat to the degradation of concrete, these earthquake-induced cracks are perforated by nature. In the corner window area subject to strong winds and rain possibly from a typhoon, there's a potential danger of leaking as the window frames are directly attached to the concrete beam. Thus, cracks in the corner window area needs to be listed as a critical check item for exterior walls inspection.

Basic Structure of High-Rise Condos

コンクリートのひび割れ　Cracks in Concrete

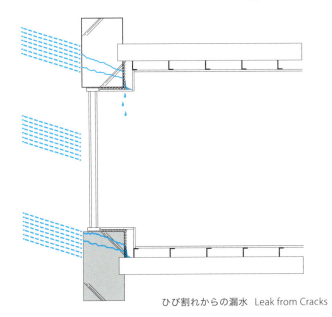

ひび割れからの漏水　Leak from Cracks

The Secrets Behind High-Rise Condos | 045

Chapter 3 タワーマンションの基本構造

タワーマンションに求められる耐震性能

タワーマンションがどの程度の耐震性能を目標に設定してきたかを示すのが右のグラフです。日本の建築基準法（188ページの「建築を取り巻く様々な法律」を参照）では最低基準が示されており、多くのマンションは、その最低基準で設計されています。しかし、タワーマンションにはより高い耐震性能が求められます。一例として、大阪地区で要求される耐震性能のレベルを右図に示しています。1980〜1990年代の関西地区では、20kine（中地震）、40kine（大地震）で設計されている建物が主流でした。これは現在の基準である25kine、50kineより20％低いものでしたが、阪神淡路大震災以降基準が引き上げられました。

このように求められる耐震性能とその基準は時代と共に変化しています。

Earthquake Resistance Performance Required for High-Rise Condos

The figure on the right page indicates the target earthquake resistance performance for high-rise condos over time. Most condos are built in accordance with the minimum requirement indicated by the Building Standards Act (see "Various Acts Around Buildings" on page 188). However, higher standards are required for high-rise condos. During the 80s and 90s, most buildings in the Kansai area were built to endure small quakes of 20 kine and large quakes of 40 kine, however, these numbers were 20 % lower than the current standards of 25 kine and 50 kine respectively revised after the Great Hanshin-Awaji Earthquake in 1995.

As seen in the figure, the seismic performance requirements and standards change over time.

Basic Structure of High-Rise Condos

耐震性能の変遷　Changing Seismic Performance over Time

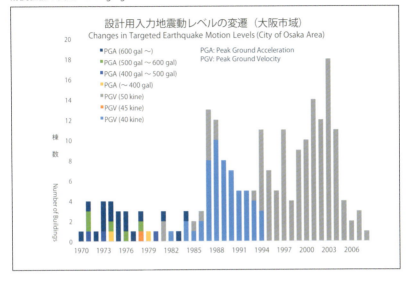

Chapter 3 タワーマンションの基本構造

耐震性の性能マトリクス

一般に設計者は、建物の規模や用途に応じて、いわゆる耐震性能のレベルを決めます。右表にその一例を示しています。Ｓクラスは原子力発電所の建屋など極めて重要な建築物、Ａクラスは丸ビルなどの大規模オフィスビル、Ｂクラスがタワーマンション向けの耐震性ということになります。その下のＣクラスが一般の建物、さらにその下のＤクラスが仮設建物などという分類になります。

Ｃクラスが建築基準法の最低レベルで、震度６強に対して建物が倒壊しないことを目標としています。ただし、再利用は想定されていません。一方、タワーマンションでは、耐震性能はＢクラス以上となり、大地震でも補修後再利用可能なレベルとなっています。最近ではコンクリートの耐用年数２００年を想定した耐震性能が、Ａクラスのタワーマンションで見られるようになりました。

オフィスビルなどでは事業主の意向に沿って耐震性が設定されます。しかしマンションでは、不動産会社などの事業者によって耐震性の目標を上げることは建設コストに直結することから、建築基準法で定められた最低基準で設定されているのがほとんどです。

耐震設計の内容の詳細は、国土交通大臣認定書（通常黒本と呼ばれる）に示されていますので、専門家であれば一目で確認、判定できます。少しでも長く住もうと考えている購入者の方は、確認しておいた方が安心かと思われます。

Performance Matrix of Earthquake Resistance

Architects generally decide the earthquake resistance grade of the building depending on its size and usage as described in the table on the right. S grade is for extremely important architecture such as nuclear reactor buildings, A for large-scale office buildings including Marunouchi Building, and B for high-rise condo buildings. Also C is for general buildings and D is for temporary houses. Grade C is the lowest level allowed by the Building Standards Act and those

Basic Structure of High-Rise Condos

buildings should not collapse in an earthquake of upper 6 class intensity, however, reusability is out of scope. On the other hand, B grade buildings including high-rise condos should be reusable possibly with some repairs even after a large earthquake. Nowadays high-rise condos with grade A quake resistance using 200-year-durability concrete started appearing.

For office buildings, the resistance grade will be determined by the requirements from the clients, however, for condos, developers including real estate companies generally use the lowest standard stated in the Building Standards Act as higher resistance means higher construction costs.

The detail of earthquake resistant design is described in the Minister of Land, Infrastructure and Transport Certificate (a.k.a. the Black Book) and any expert on architecture would understand the content at a glance. If you are planning on staying in the condo for a long period of time, I would recommend you to have some expert take a look at this.

構造駆体に関する要求性能マトリクス例 Sample of Performance Requirements Matrix for Structural Framework				
地震レベル Level of Earthquake	L1（小地震） Frequent	L2（中地震） Occasional	L3（大地震） Rare	L4（極大地震） Very Rare
再現期間（年） Return Period (yrs)	50	100	500	1000
S 最高級	無被害 Fully Operational	軽微な損傷 Operational	軽微な損傷 Operational	小破 Operational
A 高級	無被害 Fully Operational	軽微な損傷 Operational	小破 Operational	中破 Need of Repair
B 推奨	無被害 Fully Operational	軽微な損傷 Operational	中破 Need of Repair	人命保護 Near Collapse
C 一般	軽微な損傷 Operational	小破 Operational	人命保護 Near Collapse	
D 限定	軽微な損傷 Operational	中破 Need of Repair		

Chapter 3 ▌ タワーマンションの基本構造

耐震・制振・免震

もう少し耐震設計に踏み込んでみたいと思います。耐震設計は大きく三つに分類できます。骨組全体で地震時のエネルギーを吸収する耐震構造、骨組内にダンパーと呼ばれる地震エネルギーを吸収する装置を組み込む制震構造、地面から地震動そのものを受けないように積層ゴムで支える免震構造です。免震構造には基礎に免震構造を設ける基礎免震と、中間階で行う中間免震があります。

タワーマンションでは、いずれの構造形式でも国土交通大臣の認定を受けており、認定書にその設計内容が明記されています。

タワーマンションは、そもそも大きくゆっくりと揺れる構造で、地上での地震動は、一般の建物に比べ半分以下の場合がほとんどです。

タワーマンションの場合、25kine（中地震）、50kine（大地震）の大きさの地震動に対して、継続使用可、補修後使用可という目標で設計されており、これはタワーマンションとしての最低条件となっています。巨大地震が起きている昨今ではさらに上の75kineの極大地震に対して、どのような性能目標となっているかを見極めることが重要です。

中間免震のタワーマンションは、敷地が狭いことや上部構造の大幅なコストダウンを図るために採用することが多く、75kineの極大地震に対しての耐震性能に課題が残ります。

Seismic Resistance, Vibration Control and Seismic Isolation

Let's dive into the earthquake resistance design a little bit. There are basically three approaches. The first one is seismic resistance design to absorb earthquake energy in the whole framework, and the second one is vibration control to install mechanism called damper into framework in order to absorb earthquake energy there. The last one is seismic isolation to isolate earthquake motion from the ground using laminated rubber in the base or in the mid-story

Basic Structure of High-Rise Condos

and they are called base isolation and mid-story isolation respectively.
All the high-rise condos must receive a certificate from the Minister of Land, Infrastructure and Transport, and you can find the type of seismic design there.
High-rise condos, by nature from their structure, shake wider but slower, and the ground motion is usually less than half of that of other regular buildings.
High-rise condos have a design target of continuous use with or without repair against 25 kine (mid-strength) earthquakes and 50 kine (large) earthquakes. However, this is just the bottom line. Now, it would be important to find out the performance target against a giant earthquake of 75 kine.
Mid-story isolation is employed when they do not have enough space for base isolation or when they intend to reduce the construction cost of upper structure, but their seismic performance against a huge earthquake of 75 kine is yet to see.

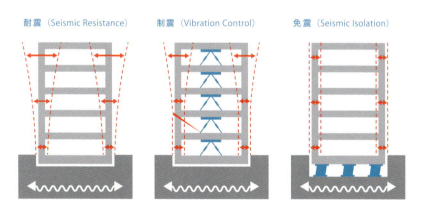

3種類の耐震設計 Three Types of Earthquake Resistance Design

Chapter 3 | タワーマンションの基本構造

無被害の構造とは

壁式鉄筋コンクリート構造という構造方式があります。これは、戦後以降目立った地震被害を受けていない方式です。

壁式構造は箱のようなもので、建物が転倒しても起こせば再利用可能な構造ですが、一般には5階以下で四角に近い形状のみとなります。

新潟沖地震の液状化（182ページの「地盤の液状化現象」を参照）で倒れた後、起こして再利用された例があります。

一方タワーマンションについては、阪神淡路大震災時の神戸ポートアイランドのタワーマンション群、東日本大震災時の仙台のタワーマンションなどは、建物の大きな被害は報告されていません。

さらなる安全性向上のため、今後はコンクリート構造物としての補修方法や、複数回の地震を受けた場合の累積の損傷などについて、研究が進むことを期待します。

Safest Structure in Past Earthquakes

A structure called box frame reinforced concrete construction has escaped serious damage from the major quakes after the WWII.

As the name indicates, a box frame structure is like a box, and even if the building tumbles, you can raise it up for reuse. Unfortunately, there are some structural restrictions that limit the building height to less than 6 stories and the shape to only square.

One famous example of such reuse is the apartment building that tumbled from the liquefaction (see "Soil Liquefaction" on page 182) by the Niigataken Chuetsu-oki Earthquake.

Also, high-rise condos such as the ones in Port Island of Kobe and the one in Sendai endured major earthquakes (i.e., the Great Hanshin-Awaji Earthquake and the Great East Japan Earthquake respectively) without getting any major

Basic Structure of High-Rise Condos

damage.

For further safety improvements, we would expect advancements in study of repair method for concrete structures and of accumulated damage from multiple quakes.

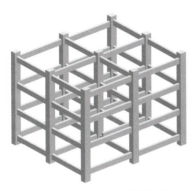 

ラーメン構造 Reinforced Concrete Structure

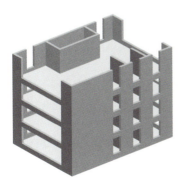 

壁式構造 Box Frame Reinforced Concrete Structure

Chapter 3　タワーマンションの基本構造

安全神話

自然災害、特に地震に対する建物の安全性には全世界共通で統計に基づいた確率論が用いられています。その確率は、今後30年間で震度6弱以上の地震がくる確率70%というような表現になります。

建物の耐震設計は、目標とする性能に対しどの程度の地震を想定し、それに対して建物の強さをどの程度にするかという作業になります。

たまに、「どんな地震がきても壊れない建物をつくってくれ」という要望を耳にしますが、残念ながら地球上に建つ限り、絶対に倒れないタワーマンションは存在しないと断言できます。壊れる確率が下がるだけです。繰り返しますが、自然災害に対して絶対安全ということは誰も言えないのです。建築基準法を守っていれば安全と思うこと自体が安全神話なのかも知れません。

Safety Myths

Safety level of high-rise condos against natural disasters is determined by the statistical probability throughout the world. And the probability description would go like: "The probably of an earthquake with seismic intensity of 6 or more in the next 30 years is 70%."

Quake resistance design for buildings is a process to determine the building strength against the projected earthquake for the targeted performance of the building.

Sometimes, people ask us to build a building that will never collapse. Unfortunately, we can say for sure that there will be no such high-rise condos as long as they are built on earth. We can only reduce the possibility of collapse. Again, there's no absolute safety against natural disasters.

To believe conformance with the Building Standards Act guarantees safety could be the safety myth.

Basic Structure of High-Rise Condos

1912年の安全神話　Safety Myth in 1912

タイタニック号では、沈没しないという前提で乗員 2,200 名の客船に対して
1,200 名程度分の救命ボートが装備がされていましたが、
事故以降は乗員数分のボート装備が義務づけられました。

Under a blind assumption for unsinkability, the Titanic was only equiped
with lifeboats for 1,200 people against the maximum capacity of
2,200 passengers and crew. After the accident,
a new regulation mandating suffficient number of lifeboats went in place.

Chapter 3 タワーマンションの基本構造

二段三段の備え

現在、如何に巨大災害から人命を守り、財産を守り、機能を維持していくかということが建築に求められています。近年、阪神淡路、東日本大震災など予想を超える大災害が起きているからこそ二段三段の備えが重要になります。

昭和56年に施行された新耐震設計法（172ページの「新耐震設計法」を参照）は、震度5程度までは建物は元の状態に戻り、震度6強程度では、元に戻らないものの、建物全体で地震のエネルギーを吸収し、倒れることなく人命を守ることを目標とする二段構えの考え方です。それまでは、設計の目標は部材が損傷しないというところまででした。新法では部材が壊れたとしても建物全体が倒壊しない設計が求められ、設計者は建物がどのように壊れるかを想定した設計をせねばならなくなりました。さらに、ダンパーなどで耐震性を向上させる三段構えの備えもあります。ただし建築基準法は、最低のレベルを示しただけのもので、実際の地震の際の性能を保証するものではありません。これらを考慮した上で実際の適切な避難計画をすれば、人命が守られる可能性は格段に向上します。

Multiple-Level Safety Measures

The current requirements for buildings are how to protect people and their property, and also to maintain functions. Now that unforeseen disasters such as the Great Hanshin-Awaji and the Great East Japan Earthquakes started hitting us, it would be important for us to prepare multiple-level safety measures.

The Building Standards Act (see "Revised Seismic Design Method" on page 172) revised in 1981 for improved seismic design proposed two-level approach. The first level is for earthquakes up to intensity 5 and building are required to go back to their original states. The second level is for earthquakes with the upper 6 intensity, and buildings should absorb the quake energy with the whole structure without collapsing in order to protect people's lives but are not

Basic Structure of High-Rise Condos

required to go back to the original states. Before the revision, architects' design goals were to avoid components from getting damaged. But after the revision, architects are required to design buildings that would not collapse even when the components are damaged. Now architects need to consider the way buildings will collapse during the design phase. Furthermore, three-level approach to improve quake resistance by using dampers in the building structure is proposed. However, the Building Standards Act just indicates the bottom line and does not guarantee actual seismic performance. When an evacuation plan is prepared properly by taking these into account, the chances of saving people's lives will greatly improve.

建築基準法の耐震基準の概要
Overview of Earthquake Resistant Design Codes Defined in Building Standards Act
Prepared by Ministry of Land, Infrastructure, Transport and Tourism (available in Japanese Only)

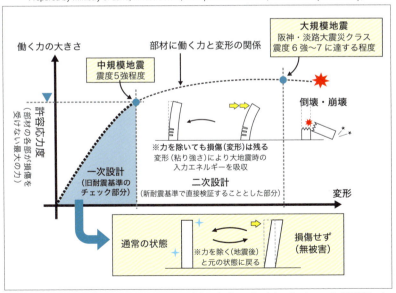

国土交通省ホームページ http://www.mlit.go.jp/jutakukentiku/house/jutakukentiku_house_fr_000043.html

Chapter 4

設計と施工
Design and Construction

Chapter 4　設計と施工

設計品質

設計と施工は、建築の品質ということでひとまとめにされていますが、求められるものがかなり違います。設計とは、真っ白なキャンバスに最初の一つの線から頭の中の形を表現する作業です。それをその通りにつくれるように図面化することが設計品質です。設計品質が最も現れやすいのは、打ち放しコンクリート仕上げです。設計者は木目など様々な模様を想定して型枠を選び、コンクリート仕様や施工方法まで特記したりします。その特記内容で設計者の力量がわかる場合があります。2016年世界遺産に登録された上野の国立西洋美術館がその代表例です。ル・コルビュジエの設計で、その弟子だった、前川國男、坂倉準三、吉阪隆正が実施設計・監理に協力していますが、柱、壁などに打放しコンクリートが多用され、60年近く経った今も美しい姿を残しています。

Design Quality

Despite often discussed together as the quality of architecture, the requirements for design and construction are quite different. Design is the process to express the form in your brain on a sheet of paper from scratch. The design quality is to prepare a drawing that guarantees the realization of the form with no error. Design quality becomes most apparent in exposed concrete finish. Architects sometimes choose wooden frameworks by taking their grain in mind and even make special notes on the concrete specs and construction method. And the special notes often reveal the ability of the architect.

The newly designated World Heritage site, the National Museum of Western Art in Ueno in Tokyo is a famous sample of the use of exposed concrete for its columns and walls. It was designed by Le Corbusier and his Japanese apprentices, Kunio Maekawa, Junzo Sakakura and Takamasa Yoshizaka helped him in detail design and administration. Even after nearly 60 years, it still maintains its beautiful appearance.

Design and Construction

ル・コルビュジエの建築物　Architecure Designed by Le Corbusier

国立西洋美術館（東京台東区上野公園内）免震構造で保存　　　　　　　　　　　Joymsk140 / Shutterstock.com
National Museum of Western Art, Tokyo, Japan

サヴォア邸　Villa Savoye, Poissy, France

ロンシャンの礼拝堂
Chapelle Notre-Dame-du-Haut de Ronchamp, France

Chapter 4 設計と施工

設計監理と設計施工

設計とは建築士が設計図を作成する業務であり、監理とは建築士が工事を設計図と照合し、確認することをいいます。設計と監理の業務を行うのが建築士事務所です。設計監理か設計施工かの違いは、設計監理を専業にしているか、あるいは「〇〇建設株式会社一級建築士事務所」のように施工会社に属しているかの違いです。

公共工事では、設計と施工が区別される設計監理が基本とされています。民間では、施工者に設計監理と施工を一括して依頼する設計施工が行われることがあります。これを責任施工と呼ぶ場合もあります。

近年、公共工事では建設物価の上昇や労務事情などから、競争入札が不調に終わることが多く、特にドームなどの特殊な大規模建築では設計内容と予算の大きな乖離が見られるようになり、その結果デザインビルドと呼ばれる方式が採用されるようになっています。これは設計段階から施工者がプロジェクトに参画する方式で、新国立競技場の設計コンペで注目されました。

しかし、施工者が設計段階から参画することでコストが先行し、設計者の斬新な発想が抑制されやすいという指摘もあります。競争原理がはたらくような建設環境のもとでは、設計と施工を分離した競争入札方式の方が透明性は高いといわれています。タワーマンションでは、施工者の持つ工法上の特許がプランや階高に影響することもあり、実際はデザインビルドのような方式となっています。設計監理と設計施工のいずれの方式でも、設計者がプロジェクトを主導し、デザインや機能を統括しているかどうかが重要です。

特に設計施工では、監理者が施工会社に属しているため、建設コスト優先の立場になることが多く、細かな部分や見えない部分でのコストダウンが行われてれしまうのも事実です。

Design and Construction

Design Administration Vs. Design and Construction

Design is a task for an architect to prepare a drawing and administration is a task for an architect to collate and check the construction with the drawing. An architect office does both design and administration. The difference between design administration and design and construction is whether the office is specialized in design administration or the office belongs to a construction company.

For public construction, design administration would be the fundamental choice to separate design and construction. For civil construction, constructor is sometimes asked to do design and construction taking care of both design administration and construction. This may be called construction with responsibility.

Competitive biddings for public construction often fail these days due to higher construction and material costs along with the labor situation. We started seeing big discrepancy between design contents and budget in special-purpose large-scale unique architecture such as a dome, and as a result, a new scheme called design-build is becoming popular. It is a method to get constructor involved from the design phase of the architecture. This approach started to draw people's attention in the design competition of the New National Stadium.

However, some people fear that the involvement of contractor from the design phase may make cost-saving their first priority and potentially discourage innovative ideas from architects. Also, it is considered to be more transparent to employ competitive bids in the construction environments where principle of competition still works.

For high-rise condos, as constructor's patents on construction method have an impact on floor height and plan, it is much closer to design-build method in reality. For either design administration or design and construction, it is important to see if the architect leads the project and oversees the design and the function. With design and construction in particular, as the administrator is an employee of the construction company, they will take the cost reduction as the first priority and they actually cut the cost in minute or inconspicuous parts of the building.

Chapter 4 設計と施工

施工会社独自の工法や施工技術

タワーマンションの施工各社は、絶えず大幅な工期短縮とコスト削減、省力化、品質向上を目指しています。今日では躯体のほとんどの部分を工場でつくり、現場では鉄筋を差し込むことで躯体はほぼ完成します。

施工法は各施工会社の特許技術であり、建築専門誌の他に一般紙などでも発表されます。特にコンクリートの強度に関する研究開発に熱心な施工会社は注目されています。これは、柱を超高強度コンクリートとした場合、地震時でもひび割れが生じにくく建物の長寿命化に貢献することがわかってきたためです。今後超高強度コンクリートのもつ重要性がさらに高まることが予想されます。

また、施工各社の系列には柱などの部材をつくる工場があり、最近では中国本土で製作することも多くなってきています。また、広大な技術研究所をもってグループ内で技術を開発し、継承していくことのできる施工会社もあります。

工法や施工技術について基礎から研究・開発に取り組んでいるかどうかは、今はネットで簡単に検索できます。「ゼネコン プレキャストコンクリート 工法」など、本書で使っているキーワードを入力すると相当数の情報にヒットします。

Construction Companies Developing Various Methods and Technologies

Construction companies building high-rise condos are continuously working towards shortening construction period, reducing costs, saving labor and improving quality. In fact, most parts of the framework are prefabricated in the plant nowadays, and there's not much left to do at the construction site other than inserting steel rods.

Construction methods are patented technologies of construction companies, and they are widely published in both industrial and general journals. The companies focusing on research and development on the concrete strength are worth paying attention to. High strength concrete will play even more

Design and Construction

important role in the future as columns built by extremely-high-strength concrete will endure earthquakes without causing cracks and thus contribute to longer lifespan of the building.

Construction companies usually manufacture building materials including columns in their affiliate companies often located in China these days. Some constructors even have huge research and development center to develop new technologies and to transfer them to the next generation.

On the net, you can easily find out who's seriously tackling the building methods and technologies. All you have to do is to enter a few keywords such as "general contractors, precast concrete, building methods" mentioned in this book into the search engine, and it will return a long list of relevant information.

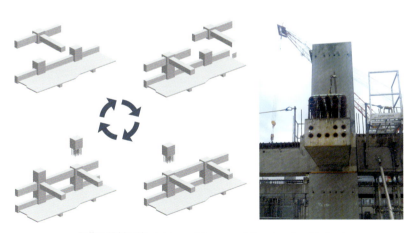

駆体の最新工法　Advanced Framework Construction Method

Chapter 4　設計と施工

品質の本質は「ひと」

大変重要なテーマですが、設計品質、施工品質を決定づける最大の要素は、やはりそこに関わる人の質ということになります。データ化された図面をコピーすれば、わずかな修正で似たような建物が次々とできていきます。林立する東京湾沿岸のタワーマンション群の中にもそのような建物は少なからず存在します。設計者が自分の言葉で建物のコンセプトや性能について、購入者に対しきちんと説明ができているかどうかが品質判断のポイントとなります。

設計者の経歴はネットなどで調べることができます。実は、建築業界、設計業界では人材のヒエラルキー（階層、ランク）があり、それは旧帝国大学や私立伝統校の建築学科を頂点とするものです。豊富な海外経験と幅広い見識で、世界中に素晴らしい建築を設計している日本の誇るべき人材を数多く輩出しています。

彼らが参画するプロジェクトには、海外の巨匠と呼ばれる建築家同様に情報や人材が集まり、「質」が必然的に高くなることは言うまでもありません。その思考過程は彼らの多くの著書から一端を知ることができます。

066 ▍ The Secrets Behind High-Rise Condos

Design and Construction

Essence of Quality - People

This is a very serious subject, but the most influential factor that determines design and construction quality is the quality of the people involved in the project. Copying the drawings from the database and making a few minor modifications there will create similar buildings one after another. As a matter of fact, there are considerable number of such high-rise condos in the Tokyo bay area. You can find this out from the clarity of the architect's statement on his/her concept and performances of the architecture.

You can look up the background of the architect on the web, but there's definitely a hierarchy of people in the construction industry with the graduates from departments of architecture of the former imperial universities and prestigious private schools at the top. Those universities are producing many outstanding talented people creating wonderful architecture all over the world with their extensive overseas experience and broad insights.

Needless to say, their projects attract information and human resource with higher quality as with the great architects of the world. You can learn a part of their design creation process from their numerous books.

Chapter 5

タワーマンションの内装
Interior of High-Rise Condos

Chapter 5 タワーマンションの内装

仕様のグレード

通常、販売価格帯によって仕様のグレードが決まってきます。

事業者、特に大手デベロッパーといわれる不動産会社などは、様々な社内基準や社内仕様をもっています。たとえば、コンセントの位置一つでも高さ25cmや45cmがあります。部屋の入り口のみ45cmという仕様もあります。これは一例ですが、その他に扉の開閉方向、廊下の幅、扉の大きさなどの仕様も事細かに決められています。

標準的な3LDKのプランでは、ほぼ各社の仕様通りとなりますが、タワーマンションでは方角とは無関係に、むしろ周辺環境やコーナー部分の眺望などで住戸の配置が決まってくることがあります。また、柱の配置も決められていることから、各階で縦方向に同じプランが連続することが多くなります。設備などの仕様のグレードについても、住戸数や販売価格から定められるケースがあります。

Interior of High-Rise Condos

Specification Grades

Generally speaking, condo's sales price determines the specification grades.
Real estate companies, so-called developers, in particular big ones, have their own standards and specifications. For example, the location of wall outlets could be 25 cm or 45 cm from the floor. Some companies use 45 cm for outlets at the room door and 25 cm for the rest. Other than this, all the details including opening/closing direction of doors, hallway width and sizes of doors are clearly specified.

All these specifications can be applied to typical three-bedroom plans. However, unit layout in high-rise condos is mostly determined, regardless of the direction of the unit, by the surrounding environment, the view from the unit corner and the face side of the neighboring building. As the column layout is predetermined in high-rise condos, it is difficult to repeat the same layout plan on the same floor. Instead, it is common to stack the same plan across the floor vertically. The specification for the equipment may be decided by the number of condo units in the building and the sale price.

Chapter 5　タワーマンションの内装

内装に見る事業者の覚悟

内装の格は建具の中でも特に引戸に現れます。最高級のタワーマンションでは、ビスなどは一切表に見えてきません。これは、ヨーロッパ系の建具に多く見られる特徴です。一方、並のタワーマンションでは、引き戸の小口にプレートとビスが見えています。修理は簡単なのですが、見た目の美しさに歴然とした差が出ます。タワーマンションでは、最近の地価や建設物価の上昇を受けて、建設費がかなりコストダウンされているため、壁はほとんどボード下地にビニールクロス仕上げとなります。その他にも、アルミサッシ、フローリング床暖房（オプション）、リビング＋対面キッチンなど、グレードの差はあれ基本仕様にそれほど差はありません。ポイントは素材です。たとえば、換気扇フードがステンレスか一般的なスチール焼付け塗装かを見ることで、事業者の意気込みがわかります。フローリングは、8年ほど前から表面を木目調にプリントされたものが普及しており、オレフィン製シートに耐摩耗性のコーティングをしたものです（198ページの「シートフローリング」を参照）。10年ほど前までは木の集成材に塗装したものが主流でしたが、竣工検査時に細かな傷が指摘されるようになってからは、表面が木製のフローリングは、タワーマンションから姿を消しつつあります。

Finding Contractor's Commitment in Interior

The interior grade is most obvious in the sliding door. In highest-grade condos, screws are nowhere to be found. This is typical with the European fixtures. On the other hand, you can easily find plates and screws on the edge of the sliding door in ordinary condos. Repairs would be easy, but they look less appealing.

Also with the higher costs of the land and the building materials, the construction cost is subject to substantial reduction. Most walls use vinyl cloth on top of backing board. Furthermore, most of the basic specifications for aluminum frames, (optional) floor heating systems, living room and open kitchen are more or less the same

Interior of High-Rise Condos

except for some grade differences. Thus, the thing to take a look at is the material. For instance, the range hood whether made of stainless steel or of bake-coated steel would show developer's enthusiasm. Floor sheets with grain printing became mainstream eight years ago (see "Sheet Flooring" on page 199). They are olefin sheets with wear resistant coating. Until 10 years ago, laminated wood with paint-coating was mostly used, however as many people found small scratches in the final inspection, that started disappearing from high-rise condos.

プレートやビスが見える引戸
Sliding Door with Plate and Screws Exposed

ステンレスの換気扇フード
Range Hood of Stainless Steel

スチール焼付け換気扇フード
Range Hood of Bake-Coated Steel

Chapter 5　タワーマンションの内装

床段差に見るタワーマンションの格

通常住戸内の床下には廊下側に繋がる配管があり、水廻りには水勾配を考慮して床スラブに段差がつけられています。この床段差は、不動産会社と建設会社のコストのせめぎ合いが見て取れる部分です。タワーマンションの床スラブは、通常工場でつくられたハーフPC (precast concrete) といわれる部材の上に現場でコンクリートを打ちます。

施工的には床スラブに段差がない方がコストがかからず、工期も短縮できますが、その分玄関の框の高さが必要になり、階段一段分の段差が出てしまいます。逆に框の高さを低くするには床スラブの水廻りに段差をつける必要があるため、躯体のコストアップにつながります。洗面台やキッチンには床下点検口がありますので、床段差があればそこから簡単に確認することができます。

玄関框の段差が50mm以下のタワーマンションは、高級と言える仕様です。

Interior of High-Rise Condos

Judging Grade of High-Rise Condos from Entrance Floor

Generally, under the floor of the residential unit, there is plumbing that leads to the hallway, and floor slabs are placed with height differences to form drainage slope for water piping. The step height between entrance and hallway is where you can see the cost reduction struggle of real estate and construction companies. Floor slabs in high-rise condos are usually made by placing concrete on top of parts called half PC (precast concrete) components fabricated in factories.

Construction-wise, it would be less expensive and quick when all the floor slabs are leveled. This, however, requires higher step between entrance and hallway. In order to reduce the step height, you need to set height differences between floor slabs and this will increase the framework construction cost. You can easily see if there are differences in the slab height through an access panel usually located in the kitchen or in the bathroom.

If the step height between entrance and hallway is less than 50 mm, you can say it's a high-grade condo.

異なる床段差
Different Step Heights at Entrance

Chapter 5 タワーマンションの内装

たかが点検口、されど点検口

タワーマンションのバルコニーに給湯器が置かれている場合は、ガス配管の点検のためにバルコニー側の壁に点検口が設けられます。またエアコンも配管接続のために点検口が設けられています。

その他、天井にも設備機器や配管の点検のための点検口がいくつか設けられている場合があります。

リビング壁に設けられている点検口は右図のようにフレームレスが基本ですが、汎用タイプが使われている場合には、コストが優先されている可能性があります。そのような仕様で事業者のデザインに対する基本姿勢を垣間見ることができます。

Access Panels – Peepholes to Quality

When a water heater is installed on a balcony of a high-rise condo, there's an access panel for plumbing inspection on the wall next to the balcony. The same thing applies to an air conditioner.

You may also find some ceiling access panels for inspecting housing equipment and plumbing.

When there's an access panel installed on the living room wall, you can tell the developer's attitudes towards design by looking at the figure on the right page.

Interior of High-Rise Condos

フレームを見せないフレームレスタイプ
Frameless Access Panel

枠を目立たなくした改良タイプ
Enhanced Access Panel with Narrower Frame

汎用タイプ
Standard Access Panel

Chapter 5 タワーマンションの内装

クロスのグレード

内装は購入者のクレーム対応となりやすいため、施工者を含めデベロッパーは、極力指摘の少ない材料を選ぶとともに、傷などの手直しが簡便でしかも安価である素材を選定します。

たとえば、布クロスは、ボードに貼る際しわが出来やすく、ある程度の職人の技量が必要になります。しかも横柄はあわせにくく、天井との境目の処理はなかなか難しいものです。

この様な材料を採用しているタワーマンションは、見えない部分でも様々な工夫がされていることが多く、価格以上の価値があるため買いに値します。クレームを少なくして早く売ろうということではなく、質の高いタワーマンションをつくるという事業者の思いがあるからです。

均質で傷の少ない内装を希望している人には、プリント柄の種類も多いビニールクロスがお勧めです。

Grades of Wall Cloth

As interior is the easiest victim of customer's complaint, developers as well as constructors tend to choose materials with better tracking record, easy to repair in case of scratches, and more importantly less expensive.

For example, wall cloth takes lots of craftsmanship to paste without creating wrinkles and the one with horizontal patterns are difficult to match at the seams and also to make adjustments at the edge to the ceiling.

If you find a condo using such cloth, it's probably a good buy as they usually put various efforts even into inconspicuous places and such a condo could be worth more than the price. They are obviously more interested in building high-rise condos with higher quality than making a quick sell by trying to minimize claims from buyers.

Interior of High-Rise Condos

However, vinyl cloth offering various patterns may be the right choice for you if you opt for uniform and scratch-free interiors.

布クロス Fabric Cloth

ビニルクロス Vinyl Cloth

Chapter 5 タワーマンションの内装

メーカーとの関係

各住宅関連のメーカーは、事業者や施工者が採用している特記仕様やマニュアル類に、自社の基準や仕様を採用してもらうため日々営業を行っています。それらは、杭、コンクリートからユニットバス、キッチン、コンセントに至るほぼすべての製品に及んでいます。各メーカーは、各事業者や施工者の営業担当を置き、新製品の紹介や見積などを作成し、商品を企画する部署に日参しています。経営改善のため事業者や施工者が合併した場合など、旧社の営業担当が生き残りをかけてこれまでよりも激しい営業合戦を繰り広げることがあります。これには販売代理店も加わってきます。

これらの行為の中で、様々な思惑がはたらくことは容易に想像できます。

ここで注意することは、同じグレードのマンションでも Ａ社仕様とＢ社仕様が大きく異なることがあり、各メーカーの営業担当は事業者、施工者各社の仕様を熟知しているため、Ａ社仕様をＢ社に対して提案することはありません。

ただし、タワーマンションでは発注規模が大きいため、大手メーカーでしか対応できないのが現実です。

Relationship with Manufacturers

Equipment manufacturers are making daily sales efforts so that their product specifications will be adopted in major developers' manuals and special specifications. Such efforts extend to pretty much all the products from piles, concrete and bath modules to kitchen components and wall outlets. Manufacturers assign developer specific salesperson and he/she would visit the product marketing section of the developer every day to introduce new products and to prepare quotes. When a merger between developers for improved management happens, such competitive activities get even fiercer for survival. At this point, some sales distributors may jump in.

Interior of High-Rise Condos

It's easy to guess all of them want to play their games.
Developers may have totally different specifications even for the condos at the same grade level. Knowing all the specifications of the developers and the constructors, salespeople from manufacturers won't make a mistake of proposing the specifications of other developers/constructors.
However, in the case of high-rise condos, only big manufacturers can handle massive quantities.

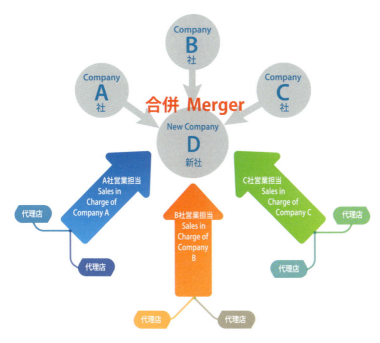

各社それぞれに何社かの代理店があり、
代理店同士で受注競争することもあります。
Furthermore, distributors of manufacturers
may compete for contracts

Chapter 6

タワーマンションの設備
Appliances of High-Rise Condos

Chapter 6 タワーマンションの設備

最新設備が採用されているかどうか

タワーマンションの施工期間は2年から3年ほどかかり、設計はそのさらに半年から1年以上前に行われます。その間住宅設備の新製品は続々と発表されますが、その発注期限は早めにやってきます。

新製品をモデルルームに反映できるかどうか、事業者の姿勢やゼネコンの力量がはっきりと現れるところです。テレビで最新設備を大々的に宣伝しているにもかかわらず、このマンションでは採用されていないというのでは少し寂しい気がします。キッチンやトイレの水栓などの汎用品は、大量購入することで事業者側にメリットが大きくなりますが、発注期限も早まります。そこで、写真のような輸入品などデザイン性を重視した製品が大量に使われていると、事業者の意気込みが伝わります。ただし、温度調節機能などデザインより性能重視の人には、国産品をお勧めします。

Use of Latest Appliances

It usually takes 2 to 3 years to build high-rise condos and the design needs to start at least a half or one year prior. During these times, new products keep on appearing, but the order cutoff cannot wait for all these new products.

Use of latest appliances is where you can tell the enthusiasm of the developer as well as the capabilities of the general contractor. It would be a bit disappointing if the widely advertised products are missing from the condo. Buying commodity devices such as kitchen and bathroom faucets in large quantity would give developers a big saving in exchange for early ordering obligation. Selection of stylish imported products listed in the opposite page would reveal developer's enthusiasm. However, Japanese products would be a good choice for you if your first priority is performance over design such as precise temperature control.

Appliances of High-Rise Condos

海外メーカー製の蛇口　Faucet Made by Foreign Manufacturer

国内メーカー製の蛇口　Faucet Made by Domestic Manufacturer

Chapter 6　タワーマンションの設備

エネルギーを見極める

タワーマンションでのオール電化は、一長一短はありますが、火災への安全性や災害時の復旧という点で優れています。電気とガスをどのように扱うかは議論のあるところですが、一棟で1,000戸を超えるような場合は、安全性を優先すべきではないかと思います。

一時期、ホテルライクな生活やサービスを提供する、24時間いつでもお湯がすぐに出る「ヒーツ」というシステムが導入され、オール電化タワーマンションとして販売されました。これは、全戸共用のガス熱源機で一括して給湯するシステムですが、設備の改修に多額の費用がかかることから、最近では導入されていません。現在では、HEMS（Home Energy Management System）という、タワーマンションでも電気、ガス共に個別に給湯設備を設置し省エネを図る方式が一般的となっています。いずれの方式でも維持管理コストを考慮する必要があります。

最近では、マンション全体でHEMSを統括するMEMS（Mansion Energy Management System）と呼ばれる電力のマネジメントシステムが開発されるなど、タワーマンションの省エネルギー対策は次の段階に進みつつあります。

Examining Utilities

There are naturally pros and cons, but all electric systems excel at safety in case of fire and at recovery from disaster. The choice between electricity and city gas is subject to open discussion, but I believe safety should come first for large-scale condos with more than 1,000 units per building.

Sometime ago, a system called HEATS (Housing Heating Total System) was introduced to some "all-electric" high-rise condos in order to provide hot water any time of the day. In reality, water was boiled by city gas and distributed to each unit. Since the system is very expensive to repair, there's no new adoption for quite a while. Now it is more common to install systems like HEMS (Home Energy

Appliances of High-Rise Condos

Management System) to manage and conserve hot water and electricity in each unit. But in any case, you need to take a close look at their maintenance and repair cost.

The energy saving measures of high-rise condos are entering into the next phase with the introduction of new power management systems such as MEMS (Mansion Energy Management System).

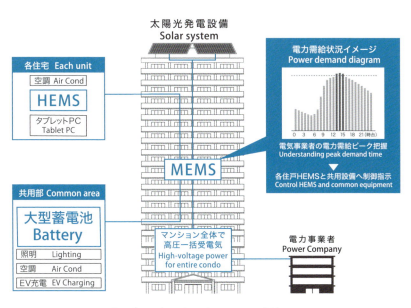

エネルギーマネージメントシステムの概念
Concept Diagram of Energy Management System

Chapter 6 タワーマンションの設備

天吊りカセット

タワーマンションでは、エアコンの取り付け方法で並か高級かに分かれます。高級マンションでは、天吊カセット（通称：天カセ）とよばれる室内機が標準装備されています。天井内のダクトの工事などは空調専門のメーカーでないと難しく、天井開口部の処理や点検口など後からかなり費用のかかる工事になるからです。

また天カセの場合、デザイン上、折り上げ天井といって中央部を高くすることがあり、躯体としての階高も必要になります。室外機も最初から設置されるので、高級マンションでは外部からは少しでも見えにくくなるように設計されています。

玄関正面に立って建物を見上げたときに、設備機器や樋などがどのように見えるかは、デザイン上検証すべき重要なポイントの一つです。

このあたりの情報は、一般にパンフレットには記載されていません。だからこそ、事業者の取り組みが問われるところでもあります。

Ceiling-Mounted Air Conditioner Package

There's a clear distinction between high-grade condos and regular ones by the way they install air conditioners. In high-grade condos, ceiling-mounted air conditioner package units come standard. It would be very expensive to switch from wall-mount air conditioners to ceiling-mounted ones as it would take some air-conditioning specialized contractor for duct work and would require additional work for cosmetic finish of the ceiling opening and access panel installation.

Also, to enhance the visual appearance, a coved ceiling-may be used. As it requires more height at the center of the ceiling, you will need additional ceiling height in the framework. In high-grade condos, developers will try to hide the preinstalled outdoor air conditioner unit from passengers' eyes as much as possible.

When you look up the building from the front entrance, you must pay attention to how the equipment, the rain pipes and the water tank look.

Appliances of High-Rise Condos

In general, such information will not be covered in the collaterals, and thus, will be a very good measure to find out the developer's commitments to design.

天吊りカセット
Ceiling-Mounted Air Conditioner Package

Chapter 6 タワーマンションの設備

換気システムのグレード

タワーマンションでは、風が強く窓を閉め切った状態にする時間が多いため、給排気システムの見極めが重要です。システムとしては、大きく A、B、C ランクに分かれますが、24 時間換気システムは必須です。

A ランク　同時給排気システム
B ランク　換気扇連動給排気
C ランク　差圧式給排気

内廊下タイプのタワーマンションでは A ランクの同時給排気システムが基本です。ただし、換気扇の給気ダクトには風量を確保するためフィルターが設けられていないので、外気が直接室内に入ってくることになります。

B ランクでは、間取りや吸気ファンの取り付け位置によって、十分な性能が得られないことがあります。

また C ランクでは、換気扇作動時に室内の圧力が下がることでドアの開閉が重くなることを解消するためパスダクトを設けたり、ドア自体に差圧解消機能を持たせて開発された玄関ドアも使われたりしています。

Grades of Ventilation System

You need to take a close look at the 24-hour ventilation system, a must in high-rise condos where windows are mostly closed because of the high wind. The ventilation system is categorized into the following 3 ranks, A, B and C:

Rank A:　Simultaneous air supply and exhaust

Rank B:　Ventilation fan synched air supply and exhaust

Rank C:　Differential pressure air supply and exhaust

Rank A will become standard for high-rise condos with internal hallways. As there's no intake filter installed in order to secure ample air flow, outside air will directly flow into the unit.

Appliances of High-Rise Condos

Rank B may not be able to achieve expected performance depending on the layout of the room and the location of the fan.

With C rank system, when a ventilation fan is in operation, lower room pressure makes it hard to open the door. This can be resolved by setting up a duct or by using a door with pressure differential reduction mechanism.

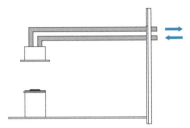

A ランク 同時給排気システム　Rank A: Simultaneous Supply and Exhaust

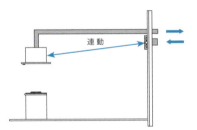

B ランク 換気扇連動吸排気　Rank B: Ventilation Fan Synched Air Supply and Exhaust

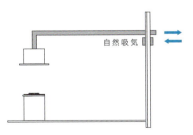

C ランク 差圧式吸排気　Rank C: Differential Pressure Air Supply and Exhaust

Chapter 6 タワーマンションの設備

維持管理等級3とは？

「品確法」（188ページの「建築を取り巻く様々な法律」を参照）によって維持管理等級3は次のように決められています。

共用部排水管

a．躯体を傷めないで排水管の更新を行うことができる。
例）共用排水管が貫通部を除き、コンクリートに埋め込まれていないこと

b．専用住戸内に立ち入らずに排水管の更新を行うことができる。
例）共用排水管が共用部分、建物外周部、バルコニーなどに設置されていること

c．共用排水管の更新時における、はつり工事や切断工事を軽減することができる。
例）分解可能な排水管の使用や新しい排水管の設置スペースをあらかじめ設けておくなど

維持管理等級が3以外の場合は、その理由をパンフレット等で確認する必要があります。計画上どうしても点検や更新に支障をきたす部分があるために、20年から30年後に予定されている共用部設備更新の際、室内仕上げや床を一部解体しての作業を伴う場合があるからです。

また、そのような配管計画では無理のあることが予想されるため、長く住み続けたいと考えている場合は維持管理等級が3以外の物件は避けた方が良いでしょう。

Grade 3 of Maintenance Control Measures

Grade 3 of maintenance control measures is defined as follows by the Housing Quality Assurance Act (see "Various Acts Around Buildings" on page 188):

Grade 3 of maintenance control measures for drain piping in the common area:

a. To be able to renew drain piping without damaging framework
ex. Common drain piping shall not be embedded in concrete except for the through piping portions

b. To be able to renew drain piping without entering residential units
ex. Common drain piping is located in common, exterior and balcony areas.

c. To be able to reduce chipping and cutting work when renewing common drain piping
ex. Use of disassemblable drain piping or reservation of extra room for new drain piping

Appliances of High-Rise Condos

If the grade is not 3, you need to find out the reason from the contractor. We could foresee inevitable issues in the future inspection and repair, and in the renewal of common area facilities, they may have to tear down the interior or the floor of the room.

Also, it would be wise to avoid such a condo with some possible plumbing issue if you are looking for a long-term residence.

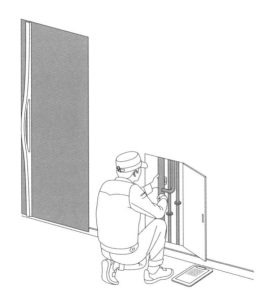

点検、更新が躯体のはつりや専用住戸内に立ち入らずに可能
Enabling Inspection and Renewal without
Chipping Framework or Entering Individual Unit

Chapter

7

タワーマンションの外構

Exterior of High-Rise Condos

Chapter 7 タワーマンションの外構

植栽計画

芝生を植えた緑のガーデンや、四季折々の花々を配した庭園は、タワーマンションのもう一つの魅力となっています。

都心に建つタワーマンションは、高さを求めて容積を積んでいくため、敷地内での広い外構計画が可能となり、造園デザイナーなどを起用して竣工当初から高木を植えた森に近い植栽をつくります。それによって生まれる街路樹と照明デザインの一体感や周辺開発とのデザインコードの統一は、タワーマンションができることで可能になり、街全体のイメージアップにもつながります。

Planting Plan

Green gardens with seasonal flowers and lawns are another appealing feature of high-rise condos.

As you would stack up stories for capacity in high-rise condos in the city center, it will leave plenty of room for exterior landscaping. Some developers hire landscaping designers so that they can prepare wood-like planting ready at the time of construction completion. A sense of unity between roadside trees and illumination design and the unification of the design codes of the areal development plan can be achieved only with high-rise condos, and this will lead to the creation of more attractive community.

Exterior of High-Rise Condos

植栽計画されたタワーマンション　High-Rise Condos with Well Planned Landscaping

Chapter 7　タワーマンションの外構

桜は高級マンションの代名詞

タワーマンションの桜のある庭園は、都心のちょっとしたオアシスです。

桜は、きちんとした管理をするかしないかで極端に寿命が変わり、それ相応の維持管理コストがかかります。

逆に、植栽に桜がないタワーマンションの場合は、当初から管理費を節約している可能性が高く、本体建物も様々なコストダウンをしている可能性があり、計画全体を慎重に見るべきだと思います。

事業主がつくるパンフレットに桜がある場合は、完成予想図などのため、むしろ強調しすぎるくらいに桜の絵が書かれているからです。

Cherry Trees Represent High-Grade Condos

A high-rise condo's garden with cherry trees is an oasis in the city center.

The longevity of cherry trees is greatly dependent on the maintenance. Poor maintenance could result in substantially short lives, and of course, good maintenance requires adequate cost.

If a condo seemingly with sufficient maintenance fund misses cherry trees, you would want to take a closer look at their overall plan as they may try to cut down the maintenance cost from the beginning as well as the building cost.

Developers usually tend to overemphasize the presence of cherry trees in the site plan renderings in their collaterals.

Exterior of High-Rise Condos

高層マンションに咲く桜　Cherry Blossoms of High-Rise Condos in Full Bloom

Chapter 7 タワーマンションの外構

風害対策のための街路樹

住宅地に忽然と姿を現すタワーマンションでは、景観や風害による近隣住民とのトラブルが多く、周辺建物などへの風害の抑制のために敷地周辺に高木を植えることがあります。環境保全のため、地域によっては建物に高さ制限が設けられたりしていますが、やはり街の景観を考えた抜本的な対策が求められます。モデルルームなどの模型と実際ではかなり印象が異なることがあります。

Street Trees to Prevent Wind Damage

High-rise condos appearing rather all of a sudden in the residential area often create conflicts with the residents in the neighborhood due to the wind damage and the changes in the scenery. Some trees around the premise are planted to minimize the wind damage to the neighboring buildings. In order to protect the environment, there are regulations in some areas to limit the height of the buildings, but more fundamental action with the overall cityscape in mind seems necessary. The miniature model in the model room sometimes looks completely different from the actual landscape on completion.

Exterior of High-Rise Condos

代表的な欅 Popular Zelkova trees

模型での表現 Model display

Chapter 7　タワーマンションの外構

メンテナンスの重要性

高木、中木、低木、四季折々の花々は、ほとんどがその土地にもともと生えていた木々ではないため、日々のメンテナンスを怠ると、急速に弱ってきます。もともと、ビル風の影響で生育には厳しい環境下にあり、樹木医による定期的な診断は欠かせません。特に、歩道に面した植栽の植え替えが必要になると、樹木費以外に、路面の掘削復旧や電線の養生費などで、一本百万円単位の費用がかかることがあります。

Importance of Maintenance

Most plants including trees, lower trees, shrubs and seasonal flowers are not native to the location and it takes daily maintenance to keep them healthy. Also as strong winds create an unfriendly environment for them, regular checkups by an arborist is an absolute must. Transplanting trees of the sidewalk could cost as much as millions of yen per piece as it may take unpaving and repaving of the sidewalk in addition to the protection of power cables.

Exterior of High-Rise Condos

日本のさまざまな植栽　Various plants in Japan

Takashi Images / Shutterstock.com

The Secrets Behind High-Rise Condos | 103

Chapter

8

タワーマンションの防災計画
Disaster Prevention Plan of High-Rise Condos

Chapter 8　タワーマンションの防災計画

地震時のタワーマンションの揺れの特徴と対策

「ゆっくり、大きく、長い時間」が特徴です。ガタガタと揺れて食器棚から食器が飛び出すという状況よりも、柱が上下に変形することで、比較的小さいと思われる地震でも床が少し傾き、食器棚自身が倒れる危険性の方が高くなります。そのため、食器棚や家具を天井や壁などに強固に固定する必要があります。突っ張り棒などの固定の際は、天井の下地の位置を確認し、設置することが重要です。また、窓際の置物などの固定も必要です。

地震時の建物外部周辺は、必ずしも安全とはいえません。ガラスやタイルの落下など生命に危険がおよぶことも考えられます。むしろ建物内に留まる方が安全です。そのためには、次の対策を講じておく必要があります。

1. 傾きに対応する。滑り防止、窓際の置物や書棚などの書物などの落下防止。
2. 出かける前は扉などを閉めるか、ドアストッパーでドアを固定する。
3. サッシは開け放しにしない。
4. サッシのクレセントは確実に閉める。
5. 防災点検は、必ず受ける。

日頃からの少しの気配りで、家財の破損や、室内での罹災を防ぐことができます。

Shaking Characteristics of High-Rise Condos in an Earthquake and Countermeasures

Quakes are slow, wide and long in high-rise condos. Thus, even in a relatively small earthquake, you will have to worry about the falling cupboards from floor tilting caused by the deformation of columns rather than the falling tableware from the cupboards. In order to prevent this, you will have to secure furniture including cupboards firmly to the wall. When using tension rods, you need to check the location of ceiling joists. Also, objects by the window need to be secured.

It may not be safe to go outside during an earthquake because of the falling objects

Disaster Prevention Plan of High-Rise Condos

like tiles and shattered glass. You'd rather want to stay inside, but you will have to take proper safety measures beforehand.

1. Prepare for tilt, and prevent furniture from slipping and objects by the window and books from falling.

2. Close the doors or secure them with door stoppers when going out.

3. Do not left windows open.

4. Use window locks

5. Do not skip disaster prevention inspection.

You can prevent injury at home and damages to your household goods with daily attention.

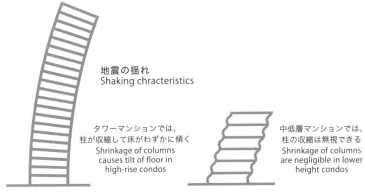

地震の揺れ
Shaking chracteristics

タワーマンションでは、
柱が収縮して床がわずかに傾く
Shrinkage of columns causes tilt of floor in high-rise condos

中低層マンションでは、
柱の収縮は無視できる
Shrinkage of columns are negligible in lower height condos

家具転倒対策チェックリスト

詳細は下記のページをご覧ください：
オフィス家具・家電製品の転倒・落下防止対策に関する調査研究委員会における検討結果について

（東京消防庁ホームページ）
http://www.tfd.metro.tokyo.jp
Information on preventing furniture falls available at this URL (in Japanese only)

Chapter 8　タワーマンションの防災計画

地震時の避難の実態

3.11 東日本大震災時のタワーマンションの状況は？
外出していたほとんどの高層階の住民、特に、赤ちゃん連れの親御さん、お年寄り、身障者の人々はロビーで夜を明かしていました。管理会社もすぐには対応できず、備蓄食料も十分に配布されませんでした。結局、エレベーターが復旧するまで、身動きの取れない状況というのが実態です。ロビーに高価な応接セットなどが置かれている高級マンションほど、横になるような家具は置かれていません。今後はこのようなインテリアについても十分な検討が必要となるとともに、災害時の会議室などの共用部の利用方法を決めておくことも重要です。

Disaster Prevention Plan of High-Rise Condos

What Really Happened When an Earthquake Took Place

What happened at high-rise condos on March 11, 2011 when the Great East Japan Earthquake took place?

Residents who were outside of the building, particularly parents with a baby/babies, the aged and the disabled, had to stay overnight in the lobby. Maintenance companies also had a hard time in handling the situation and could not provide emergency supply. After all, they could not do much until elevators resume operation. Condos with expensive lounge furniture do not usually offer temporary bedding, but we need to do something about this in the future and it would be important to decide a few things including the way to utilize the common area such as meeting rooms in an emergency.

Chapter 8 タワーマンションの防災計画

避難安全検証法とは？

一般的には、タワーマンションの防災計画は、構造と同様に防災評定という国土交通省の認定を取得しています。

認定で用いられる避難安全検証法とは、建物内の在館者が一定時間内に外部など安全な場所に移動できるかどうかをシュミレーションする方法です。

いくつかの計算方法があるのですが、それらは専門書に譲ることとして、ここで問題として挙げたいのは、この方法が健常者を前提とし、身体障害者などは考慮されていないということです。つまり、避難時の移動が階段利用を前提とされ、車椅子での避難は考慮されていないのです。

さらに、消防法により火災検知器、スプリンクラー等の消火設備の設置が義務づけられています。これらの日頃からの点検が重要なことはいうまでもありませんが、消火設備の点検実施率は7割を超えていれば優秀な方です。

いざという時のために、非常用発電機の電源供給範囲や作動時間、燃料の供給方法も確認しておく必要があります。

Verification Method for Evacuation Safety

High-rise condos generally receive a certificate from Ministry of Land, Infrastructure, Transport and Tourism for their disaster prevention plan.

A methodology called Verification Method for Evacuation Safety is used in this certification process to simulate whether the expected occupants of the building are able to move to some safe place possibly outside within a certain period time.

There are several ways of simulation, but we do not go into detail. The problem here is their assumption that excludes the disabled. Also, since use of stairs is assumed, there's no evacuation guidance for wheelchairs.

On the other hand, Fire Service Act requires deployment of firefighting equipment including fire alarms and sprinklers. Regular inspection of such equipment is very

Disaster Prevention Plan of High-Rise Condos

important, but in reality, the inspection coverage rate over 70 % would be considered excellent.

Just in case, it would be necessary to find out the coverage area of the emergency power generator and its hours of operation as well as the fueling procedure.

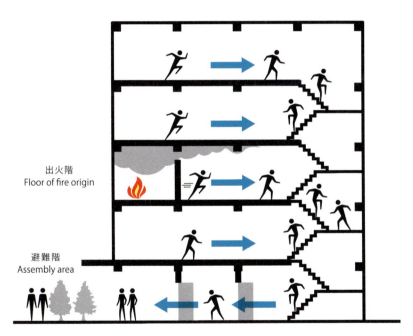

全館避難安全性能のイメージ図 Performance of Evacuation Safety for Entire Building

Chapter 8　タワーマンションの防災計画

住戸内火災の避難のポイント

タワーマンションの防火対策は、建築基準法、消防法の二段構えになっています。建築基準法により、煙を建物外に強制的に排出する強力な排煙設備と、火や煙の拡散を防ぐ防火扉などが備えられています。一方、消防法によって定められたとおり、警報が鳴るとともにスプリンクラーが作動し、連結送水管を使った消火活動が行われます。しかし、地震の影響などで、防火扉の枠が曲がったり、特別避難階段のALC壁（200ページの「ALC パネル」を参照）が欠けてしまったりして、その機能を十分に発揮できない場合も考えられます。毎年の管轄消防署の消防点検では、すべての防火扉やALC板の検査をするわけではないので、管理会社の点検状況を確認する必要があります。

防火防煙設備が適切に作動すれば、地震同様、慌てず室内に留まり、非常放送などで状況を確認してから避難するというのが賢明です。

地震、火災ともに、日頃から外部との連絡方法や情報収集の方法、避難の方法などを確認しておくことは、タワーマンションに暮らす上で重要であるのはいうまでもありません。

Evacuating from Fire at Condo Unit

Fire prevention measures for high-rise condos are a dual scheme regulated by both the Building Standards Act and the Fire Service Act.

By the Building Standards Act, powerful smoke exhaust systems to discharge smoke out of the building and fire doors to prevent fire and smoke from spreading are installed. Also by the Fire Service Act, fire alarms will ring and sprinklers will start, and firefighting will start through connected water conveyance pipes. However, warped fire doors and chipped ALC panel walls (see "ALC (Autoclaved Lightweight Concrete) Panels" on page 200) in the emergency stairs damaged by an earthquake or other incidents will degrade the performance of the fire prevention system. Since your fire

Disaster Prevention Plan of High-Rise Condos

station will not inspect all fire doors or ALC panels in their annual fire inspection, it would be necessary to check how your maintenance company conducts their inspections.

If all the fire and smoke proof equipment is fully functional, it would be wise to stay in the room for the time being and follow the emergency instruction announcements.

In order to live in a high-rise condo, it is critical that you acquaint yourself with the way to contact outside and to collect necessary information as well as the evacuation procedure.

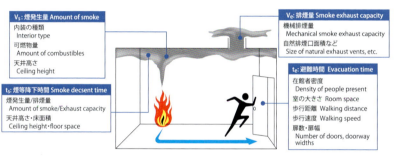

安全な避難のための建築基準法 Building Standard Ac for Safe Evacuation

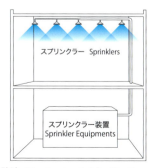

防火・消火のための消防法 Fire Service Act for Fire Prevention & Extinguishing

Chapter 8 タワーマンションの防災計画

タワーマンションでの避難方法

結論からいうと、地震時は室内に留まるのが最も安全です。火災時の避難で使う特別避難階段は必ずありますが、タワーマンションでは一般に低層階の損傷が大きく、外部に出ると落下物などで被災する危険性が高くなるからです。

災害に備えて、地震時や火災時の状況を予想して、その上で安全確保に向けて行動するなど、避難方法を把握しておくことが重要です。東京都の防災ホームページなどで日頃から防災に関する予備知識を学んで、落ち着いて行動することを心がけて下さい。

Evacuation in High-Rise Condos

During an earthquake, it would be safest to stay in the room in high-rise condos. Of course, they have evacuation stairs, but damages are generally bigger in lower floors and there's a greater risk of getting hurt by falling objects if you go outside.

It is extremely important to learn what to do in the case of earthquake or fire. Please go through the disaster prevention scheme stated in various publications carefully and try to act calmly should a disaster happen.

Disaster Prevention Plan of High-Rise Condos

The Secrets Behind High-Rise Condos | 115

Chapter 9

購入者としての見極めポイント
Checkpoints for Purchase

Chapter 9　購入者としての見極めポイント

タワーマンションの魅力を演出する不動産会社

様々な課題をかかえつつも、売れに売れているタワーマンション。なぜでしょうか。それは、これまでのマンションにはない魅力があるからです。

遥か遠くまで見渡せる眺望、宮殿を思わせるような豪華な玄関、ゲストルーム、フィットネス、会議室などの共用施設、大規模開発ならではのゆとりある敷地を利用した外構植栽、交通の利便性や周辺インフラの整備、それらにも増して威風堂々とした外観があります。これらハード面ばかりではなく、相続税対策やインバウンドの投資対象にもなり、今や完全に時流に乗った感があります。

施工者は、高度な技術力を擁して大量生産し、プレハブ化を進め、相対的な労務費削減、基準階の繰り返しによる効率化を図ることによって、利益を生みやすくしています。また、事業者にとっても販売エリアが広く、購入者も含めた三者の利害が一致するところでもあります。

周辺の大規模ショッピングセンターとの一体開発、それに伴うインフラの整備、その他アメニティ施設の建設など、2年もすると周辺の風景が一変してしまいます。

その上、予算に応じた様々なプランや比較的低く設定された管理費、24時間の警備とゴミ出し等、これまでにない数々のサービスもあります。一度は住んでみたい。そんな思いがタワーマンションの魅力になっているのです。

Checkpoints for Purchase

Realtors to Emphasize Charms of High-Rise Condos

Despite of various challenges, high-rise condos are in great demand because of their unique features that conventional condos could not offer.

A spectacular long range view, a palace-like entrance and shared facilities like guest rooms, a fitness gym and meeting rooms, exterior planting taking advantage of spacious premises, convenient access, nearby facilities and most of all, grand appearance. Together with such physical attractiveness, economical motivations such as inheritance tax saving and investments from abroad are creating the big demand for high-rise condos today.

Constructors are better positioned for profitability now by reducing the labor cost with mass production using their advanced technologies, promotion of prefabrication, and efficiency improvements from repetitive construction of the reference floor. Also, developers can extend their sales area. Thus, constructors, developers and buyers will be all happy.

The construction is often accompanied by a development of a shopping center, infrastructure improvements and construction of other amenities. All of these will change the landscape of the neighborhood completely in a matter of two year or so.

Also, they offer novel services including the availability of various floor plans to meet your budget, relatively low maintenance fee, 24-hour surveillance and garbage stations. All of these make high-rise condos even more attractive.

Chapter 9 購入者としての見極めポイント

モデルルームは事業主のアピールの舞台

ここでは、モデルルームの見極め方を幾つかご紹介します。

見極めポイント1　営業担当者の身だしなみ

見極めポイント2　質問内容に対する真摯な対応

見極めポイント3　パンフレット類の質

見極めポイント4　耐震性や改修のしやすさなどの売りの部分を確認する

見極めポイント5　設計変更、メニュープランがどうなのか

最近では、ほとんどが事前予約制となっているため、モデルルームで最初に名刺を渡された営業担当者が、その後の契約、引渡しまで付き合うことになります。身だしなみや説明など、事業主の物件に対する姿勢が現れるところです。マニュアルに沿って一方的に説明を進めるような担当者では、柔軟な対応が難しくなる可能性があります。

パンフレットの経費を削減しているような物件では、建築工事も様々なコストダウンをしている可能性があります。

モデルルームの内装や備品は、購買欲をかき立てる様々な工夫がされています。設計変更や、メニュープラン、オプションなどがふんだんに盛り込まれています。どこまでが無償で変更可能か、確認することが後々のトラブルを避けることにつながります。また、オプションで気に入ったものがあったら、調度品全体を考えて家具などを選ぶと、後々調和の取れた空間になります。

Model Rooms – Developer's Theater

We will go over several key points to pay attention to when you visit the model room.

Key point 1: Salesperson's attire

Key point 2: Sincerity in answering

Key point 3: Quality of collaterals

Checkpoints for Purchase

Key point 4: Sales points such as earthquake resistance and ease of repair
Key point 5: Design customization and alternative floor plans

As model room visit is mostly by appointment only these days, the salesperson who greets with you first in the model room will work with you all the way from the contract to the handover. The way the person dresses and explains is the reflection of the developer's sincerity about the property. If the person just keeps on explaining just by following the manual without listening to you, he/she may not be able to handle your request in a flexible manner.

If they hand out a cheap looking pamphlet to you, you need to be cautious as they may be cutting down the construction cost as well.

The developer tactfully prepares the interior and the fixtures of the model room to put you in the mood for purchasing. Also you have numerous choices for design modification, alternative floor plans and options, and you want to make sure what are the free options and what are not to avoid future troubles. Also, you should choose your option with overall furnishings in mind to make your space well coordinated.

Chapter 9　購入者としての見極めポイント

内覧会チェックポイント

言うまでもなく、内覧会はユーザーにとって、仕上がり具合を確認する最初で最後の機会です。しかし、ほとんどのユーザーは、クロスや床の傷や汚れを指摘しているだけで、完成した建物の性能を確認するという作業を行っていないのが実態です。インスペクターと呼ばれる建築の専門家を内覧会に同行させるユーザーもいますが、既に契約が済み、最終の入金間近であれば、よほどのことがない限り、そのまま入居をむかえることになります。

もう一度考えてみて下さい。限られた時間の中で何をチェックすべきかを。

傷や汚れは、品質そのものではありませんが、品質を表現しています。工期に余裕のない現場の仕上がり具合では、必然的に品質の低下を意味します。何とか取りつくろっても、早ければ1ヶ月後に問題が表面化してしまいます。

内覧会では建築の質を見極める幾つかのポイントがあります。

1. ユニットバス天井点検口から躯体のひび割れの状況などを確認する。
2. 壁の点検口から断熱材の施工状況を確認する。
3. 建物精度、特に壁の傾きを確認する。
4. 廊下のメーターボックスから設備とその周辺の防水、防火区画の処理状況を確認する。
5. 防火・防犯設備を確認する。
6. 手すり高さ、床段差、ドアの開閉制限などを確認する。

入居後にトラブルにならないためにも、上記のポイントは押さえておきたいものです。一般にタワーマンションの場合は、入居後に専属のアフターサービス窓口が館内に設けられますので、その際の対応方法を確認して帰るのがスマートかもしれません。

Checklist for Preliminary Inspection

Everyone knows preliminary inspection is the first and the last opportunity for users to inspect the finished condo unit. However, most users just point out scratches and stains on the wall and the floor without checking the performance of the building.

Some people even bring in an expert on architecture called inspector. But now that contract is closed and you are about make a payment, it's highly likely that you will just move in unless there's something serious.

Please reconsider what to look at in the limited time of inspection.

Scratches and stains do not directly represent the quality themselves but have something to do with the quality level. Under tight construction schedule, the finished quality will definitely go down. They may be able to cover it up for a while, but you will find the problem within a month at the earliest.

There are several things to pay attention to in inspection to avoid troubles after move-in:

1. **Inspection panel in the bathroom ceiling –**
   To check things like cracks in the building frame.

2. **Inspection panel on the wall – To check how insulation materials are placed.**

3. **Building precision, particularly floor**

4. **Meter box in the hallway –**
   To check facilities and waterproofing and fireproofing around them.

5. **Fire and crime prevention measures**

6. **Safety measures including handrail height, floor level difference, door stoppers**

Since, in high-rise condos, there will be a dedicated service representative inside the building, it may be wise to talk to that person to find out how to get the support after move-in.

Chapter

10

維持管理の重要性
Importance of Maintenance and Management

Chapter 10 維持管理の重要性

管理組合の役割

竣工引渡し後、建物の維持管理は、区分所有法（190ページの「区分所有法」を参照）にもとづき、区分所有者全員からなる管理組合にゆだねられます。管理組合理事会が様々な管理運営にかかわる事項を決議していきます。

ここで問題となるのは、毎年抽選や立候補で選任される理事の中に、タワーマンションの専門家がほとんどいないということです。最近、外部理事を選任することを認める運用が可能になりましたが、実際の運用にまでは至っていないのが現状です。例えば、タワーマンションの修繕は日々必要な業務で、少しでも怠ると急激なコンクリートの劣化の進行やシールからの漏水が至るところで起こります。管理組合には、専門的知識を持った、本当の意味でのモラルの高い専門家が求められます。

Role of Owners' Maintenance Association

By the Unit Ownership Act (see "Building Unit Ownership Act" on page 190), the maintenance of the building will be handed over to the owners' maintenance association comprising of all the unit owners after the completion and handover of the condo unit, and the association board will decide various things related to the maintenance and management of the building.

The problem here is that there are very few experts on high-rise condos among the directors selected annually by drawing or voting. Recently it became possible to invite outside board members, but not too many associations operate that way yet. Maintenance of high-rise condos is necessary every day, and if failed, a disaster such as concrete carbonation and sealing leak will happen all over the place. We need an expert of truly high morals to avoid such a situation.

Importance of Maintenance and Management

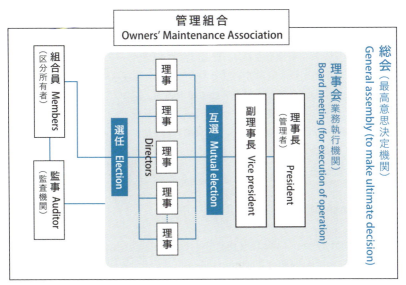

事業者が作成する管理規約で定められています
Organization Defined in Management Bylaw Prepared by Developer

Chapter 10 ┃ 維持管理の重要性

長期修繕計画の重要性

売買時の長期修繕計画は、修繕積立金の算定根拠に過ぎないということを理解していないと、後々管理会社や事業者との意見がかみ合わなくなることがあります。竣工後の適切な維持管理の主役は、管理組合です。タワーマンションの維持管理では、様々な専門知識や経験が必要となり、区分所有者への的確な説明も求められます。長期修繕計画は、管理会社の協力の下、建物の修繕状況を考慮して、定期的に見直すことが必要です。

また、専門家である元設計者、元施工者と理事会が長期にわたる良好な関係を保ち、資産価値を維持できる体制作りをすることも重要です。

Importance of Long-Term Repair Plan

If you are not aware of the fact that the repair plan presented at the time of purchase is just a basis for calculating the reserve fund, you may have a hard time in the future discussions with the maintenance company and the developer.

After the completion of construction, owners' maintenance association will take over the responsibility for maintenance. Maintenance of high-rise condos requires various expertise and experiences. Also, accurate explanation to the owners is mandatory. Long-term repair plan should be reexamined periodically with a help from the maintenance company by taking the current repair status into account.

It would be equally important for the board of directors to build good relationship with the experts including the original architect and the constructor to establish a system that maintains the property value.

Importance of Maintenance and Management

本格化する大規模マンションの改修
1st Generation Large-Scale Condos About to Receive 1st Major Repair

郊外型面開発大規模マンション
Suburban Center Large-Scale High-Rise Condos

第2回大規模修繕工事
2nd Major Repair

都心大規模超高層マンション
City Center Large-Scale High-Rise Condos

第1回大規模修繕工事
1st Major Repair

基本設備の更新
Update of fundamental equipment

建替 Rebuild

容積率アップ
Increase floor area ratio

管理組合の合意形成
Consensus formation in
maintenance association

区分所有法
Building Unit
Ownership Act

主に建築工事
Mainly construction work

瑕疵担保期間
Defect Warranty Period

準備期間
Preparation Period

修繕積立金の増額
急激な躯体劣化
設備の更新
Repair fund payment hike
Rapid framework deterioration
Equipment updates

修繕 Repair

改修、リニューアルにより
資産価値の維持向上
Maintain or improve asset
value by repair and renewal

大規模修繕委員会等
管理組合が主体
Maintenance Association
to Take Leading Role

事業主による検査・是正
Inspection & Rectification by Developer

Chapter 10 | 維持管理の重要性

大規模マンションの修繕会計

一般に、事業者は管理費の負担を少なくして買いやすくすることを考えます。タワーマンションの購入時の時点では、せいぜい10年毎の長期修繕計画を20年後程度までしかたてていません。そして入居後に、管理組合総会資料などで、30年先の修繕会計を目の当たりにして、誰もが驚きます。30年先、つまり3回目の修繕積立金が大幅に不足するのです。その頃は建物の減価償却期間47年が近づき、固定資産税は下がっています。修繕積立金を順次値上げすることで、3回目、4回目と続く、大規模修繕に備えることができます。また、入居時に修繕積立金を高くして将来に備えるという考え方もありますが、一時金として集まった億単位の資金を世代を超えて国債などに預けておくのが良いかどうかは、議論の余地があると思います。

Repair Cost Accounting for Large Scale Condos

In general, developers try to make the purchase easier by lowering the maintenance cost. At the time of purchasing a high-rise condo, their repair plan is at a 10-year interval and for the next 20 years at most. After moving in, everyone gets shocked looking at the repair cost after 30 years in the general meeting materials. Reserve fund for the third repair will fall very short. Here's an idea. Some people may like it and others may not, but we might be able to increase the reserve fund payment gradually to prepare the third and the fourth repairs because the property tax after 30 or 40 years will be lower approaching to the end of depreciation period. Alternative is to raise the upfront reserve fund payment, but we need think about whether it's a good idea to save hundred-million-yen level of fund as government bonds across generations.

Importance of Maintenance and Management

長期修繕計画　Long-Term Repair Plan

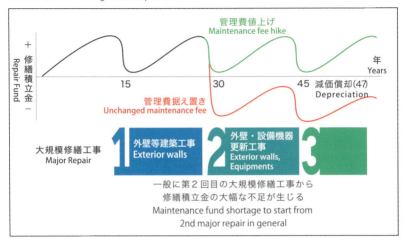

Chapter 10 維持管理の重要性

タワーマンションの駐車場

タワーマンションの駐車場には、大きく分けると自走式と機械式があります。タワーマンションが大規模化する中で、内部の空間を有効に使ったタイプが主流になっていますが、敷地に余裕のある場合は、駐車場棟を別に設けている場合もあります。設置台数については、いくつかの都心の新築マンションでは、住戸数に対して30％程度と附置義務台数に近づいてきています。

これくらいのパーセンテージになると、駐車場代の管理費への組込みや機械式駐車場の修繕費、取り替えの際の費用などの考え方にも影響が出てきます。管理組合と管理会社が協力して、将来の利用予測などをもとに、住民の意見を集約しておく必要があります。

Parking Garage of High-Rise Condo

There are two major types of parking garage in high-rise condos, self-parking and mechanical parking. As the size of high-rise condos explode, the parking system utilizing internal space is becoming the mainstream. When the site has plenty of room, a dedicated parking building can be built separately. Also the parking capacity is approaching the targeted on-site capacity requirement of 30 % of the number of units in some newly built high-rise condos in the city center.

Such high percentage will affect the way we consider the possibility of incorporating parking cost into maintenance cost, repair or renewal cost of mechanical parking structure. Owners' maintenance association and the maintenance company should collaborate to summarize the inputs from the residents along with the future use estimates.

Importance of Maintenance and Management

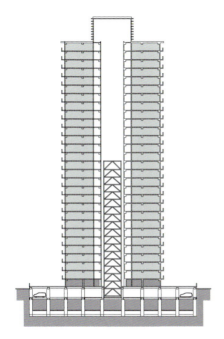

タワーマンションの駐車場
Parking Garage of High-Rise Condos

Chapter 10 維持管理の重要性

ゴミ収集問題

一般にタワーマンションでは、24時間ゴミ出しが可能です。これはタワーマンションの魅力の一つでもあります。各階にゴミ置き場が設けられ、分別収集や粗大ゴミの処理のルールのもとで行われることが前提となっています。しかし、住民の中には24時間どんなゴミでも出せると思っている人々が少なからずいます。外国人の場合はなおさらで、分別は、管理会社の仕事と思っている住民もいますが、これは大きな間違いです。ゴミ収集は地方自治体の仕事なので、粗大ゴミの回収の時に処理シールが貼られていないものは回収されません。医療系廃棄物も同様です。

ゴミは資源という考え方が根付きつつある日本ですが、あくまでも分別が前提となっていることをPRする必要があります。

かつての高度経済成長期には、日本人は廃棄物を垂れ流し、公害問題を引き起こしていました。しかし、資源の乏しい日本ゆえ、廃棄物を再利用することで資源化して循環させることが法律で定められ、ゴミの分別回収が推進されています。容器包装リサイクル法では、ペットボトルや燃えるゴミと燃えないゴミの分別が定められています。ポイントは以下の条文にあります。

「容器包装に係る分別収集及び再商品化の促進等に関する法律（平成7年6月施行）
（事業者及び消費者の責務）
第四条 事業者及び消費者は、繰り返して使用することが可能な容器包装の使用、容器包装の過剰な使用の抑制等の容器包装の使用の合理化により容器包装廃棄物の排出を抑制するよう努めるとともに、分別基準適合物の再商品化をして得られた物又はこれを使用した物の使用等により容器包装廃棄物の分別収集、分別基準適合物の再商品化等を促進するよう努めなければならない。」

192ページにリサイクル法について掲載しましたので、ご参照ください。

Importance of Maintenance and Management

Garbage Collection Issues

In high-rise condos, you can take your garbage to the garbage station designated on each floor any time of the day. This is one of the advantages of living in a high-rise condo, but you are asked to follow the rule of sorting your garbage and handling of bulky garbage. However, some residents believe they can dispose any garbage any time of day. Especially there are some people, particularly foreigners who are not familiar with the Japanese system, believing maintenance company is responsible of sorting garbage, but this is a big mistake. Garbage collection is a business of your local government and they will not collect your bulky garbage unless paid processing tickets are attached. This applies to medical waste as well.

Japanese people these days started to understand that waste could be recycled as resource, but we should emphasize the fact that sorting is the first step.

In the days of high economic growth period, Japanese people used to ignorantly discharge wastes and caused pollution all over the place. However, being poor in natural resources, Japan introduced legislation to recycle waste for reuse and to promote sorted collection of waste now. Containers and Packaging Recycling Law requires sorting of PET bottles, burnables and non-burnables. The following is a good summary of this.

Act on the Promotion of Sorted Collection and Recycling of Containers and Packaging (Enacted in June, 1995) (Responsibility of Business Operators and Consumers)
Article 4: Business operators and consumers shall endeavor to reduce waste containers and packaging discharged through rationalization of use of containers and packaging by using recyclable containers and packaging and reducing the excess use of containers and packaging. Business operators and consumers shall also endeavor to promote the sorted collection of waste containers and packaging and recycling, etc. of waste containers and packaging that conform to the sorting standards through use, etc. of things obtained by recycling waste containers and packaging that conform to the sorting standards or things using such things.

Please refer to page 192 for various recycling regulations in Japan.

The Secrets Behind High-Rise Condos ▌135

Chapter 10　維持管理の重要性

LED化の現状

現在の新築タワーマンションでは、ほぼLED照明が採用されていますが、少し前に建てられたタワーマンションでは、LDE化による電力コストの削減が進んでいないのが現実です。その理由はいくつかあります。

1. そもそも進め方がわからない。照明コンサルタントやメーカーに検討依頼するにも、その依頼先の選定方法を決めることで時間がかかる。

2. 電力削減効果が保証されない。電球だけを交換する場合は、消費電力だけでの比較はできるが、照明器具自体の劣化などで計算通りには行かないこともあり、省エネ目標の数値がメーカー毎にバラバラで、結論を出しにくい。

3. 管理組合の意思決定に時間がかかり過ぎる。タワーマンションには、千個単位の電球があり、調査、見積を含め、1年以上の時間がかかることがある。さらに、毎年入れ替わる管理組合の理事から様々な意見が出され、その度に新たな検討を要することになる。

4. まだ技術的課題が多く、メーカ間で異なる色温度や既存の電球とは違う色調のため、見る人によってさまざまな意見がでる。また、調光LEDで電気を絞っていった場合に、明るさが滑らかに変化しなかったり、赤みが出ないなど、白熱電球の調光の再現ができないなどの課題がある。

今後、更に建築に省エネルギー化が求められる中、多くのエネルギーを消費するタワーマンションも規制の対象となることが十分予想され、電気料金の大幅な減少が見込めるLED化について、事前に準備しておくことが必要です。

各種LED電球　Various LED Lamps

Importance of Maintenance and Management

On LED Lighting Deployment

Almost all new high-rise condos are equipped with LED lighting. In older high-rise condos, they are not making much progress in cutting down electricity bill by installing LED light bulbs. The reasons are as follows:

1. They don't know how to proceed to start with. Even deciding how to choose an lighting consultant and a manufacturer takes a long time.

２．There's no guarantee for cost reduction. They can compare the power consumption, however, things will be more complicated if you consider their lifetime. Also, the fact manufacturers use different measures for power reduction target makes it hard to draw a conclusion.

３．It takes too long to draw a resolution from owners' maintenance association. High-rise condos use thousands of light bulbs and it often takes more than a year to conduct an investigation and to get a quote. Furthermore, the directors of owners' maintenance association re-elected every year usually have different opinions that require examination each time.

４．Also, LEDs still have technical issues. Color temperatures are different between manufacturers. None of them look like traditional light bulbs, and people have different preferences. When used with dimmers, unlike light bulbs, they will not dim smoothly or will lack redness.

Further energy saving will be required in the future and high-rise condos with large energy consumption are a likely target of future regulations. Thus, it is necessary to consider the switch to LEDs for lower electricity consumption.

色温度の異なるLED照明　LED Illumination at Different Color Temperatures

Chapter

11

管理会社を見極める
Examining Maintenance Companies

Chapter 11 管理会社を見極める

管理会社の姿勢

建物引渡し後は管理組合が作られ、事業者関連管理会社が管理運営を行っています。1年後に管理会社が交代することもあれば、高い専門性を発揮してタワーマンションの大規模修繕工事を請け負う管理会社もあります。

日常の管理、清掃や警備業務、設備点検業務は、それぞれの専門会社を何社か集めて、見積合せを行い決めるので、比較的定型的作業になりますが、建物や設備の点検記録を確実に残すことはなかなか難しく、管理会社が過去の点検記録を探すのにかなり苦労することがあります。

これは、IT化の進め方が問題なのですが、建築業界は、書類管理を含めてデジタル化の遅れている業界のひとつであることに間違いありません。

タワーマンションには、住戸情報を含め膨大な施工記録が存在します。これらの中から図面などを効率よく、必要なときにすぐに引き出せる管理会社であれば、長く付き合う価値があると思われますが、消防点検記録一つ出すのに何日もかかるようでは、早急に改善を求める必要があるといえます。

また、管理会社の正社員が何名いるかということも、そのマンション管理への事業者の意気込みの表れでもあり、評価のポイントの一つです。

Examining Maintenance Companies

Attitudes of Maintenance Company

After the handover, owners' maintenance association will be formed and developer's affiliate maintenance company will take care of maintenance administration. After one year, some maintenance companies will become subject to replacement while others with high expertise will move on and even receive a contract for large-scale repair work of the high-rise condo.

Companies for daily maintenance, cleaning and security works, and facility inspection will be rather mechanically determined by competitive estimates between a few vendors. However, it would be very difficult to keep track of all the inspection records of the building and the facility, and the maintenance company may have a hard time in finding the required record from the past.

Adoption of IT (information technology) is the key, but construction industry is one of the late adopters even for electronic document management.

There's enormous amount of data for high-rise condos including individual unit information. If your maintenance company can readily provide you with the necessary information such as the drawing of your unit, they deserve a long-term contract. On the contrary, if it takes days for them to find some fire inspection record, you should ask for a prompt improvement.

Also, the number of the maintenance company's permanent employees is a good measure of developer's commitment to the maintenance task.

Chapter 11 管理会社を見極める

管理の質とは

管理会社は、毎年契約の更新をし、その度に重要事項説明を行い、日々奮闘しています。特にタワーマンションでは、様々な業種の人々が暮らしているので、要望やクレームも多種多様です。それらに対し適切な対応ができる人材を確保できているか、管理会社のスタッフをバックアップする体制ができているかを見極めなくてはなりません。

警備を例にとると、タワーマンションのほとんどが24時間警備になっているため、警備員が常駐しています。その分コストは上がりますが、警備会社から様々な提案を引き出し、より効率的な運営をするために本社と連絡を取り、絶えず改善に努めているかといった点を、管理会社が毎年行う重要事項説明の際に確認できれば、長く付き合う価値はあると思います。管理委託費の交渉で、管理会社に対して値下げ要求するという方法では、適正な維持管理はなかなか難しく、複数年契約などを含めて委託する管理内容を吟味する必要があります。

タワーマンションでは、修繕を確実に実施することが建物の長寿命化に直結しますが、日々の修繕履歴を大規模修繕に反映するためのデータベースの整備には、それなりのコストがかかります。

タワーマンションの管理会社の技術力を知るポイントは、大規模修繕工事を請負っているかどうかということがあります。一般のマンションとは違い、工事金額、工事規模は大きく、そこでは一級建築士などの資格を有した技術者も必要になります。今や、管理会社も技術力を売りにする時代になっているのです。また、協力会社との価格交渉能力も管理会社を見極めるための重要な要素です。

平成25年の国土交通省の資料によると、20階以上のマンションの管理費の内の修繕積立金の平均は206円/m²となっていますが、平均を超えるタワーマンションのほとんどが都心高級マンションです。

Examining Maintenance Companies

Quality of Maintenance

Maintenance companies, in addition to their daily work, explain important matters at their annual contract renewal. And since they are getting a diversity of requests and claims from wide range of residents living in high-rise condos, you want to make sure whether their representative is capable of handling all of these and whether they have a backup system in place to support the staff of the company.

Let's take the security as an example. Most of high-rise condos offer 24-hour security and guards are stationed all the time. This comes at a price, but it would be worthwhile if you can confirm, at the annual explanation meeting hosted by the maintenance company, their continuous efforts to make improvements through various proposals and collaboration with the maintenance company for more efficient operations. Requesting a service fee reduction alone will not do anything good in getting a proper maintenance service. Instead, you will need to look closely at the contract detail including the possibility of a multi-year contract.

It is extremely important to conduct repairs to extend the lifespan of the building, but developing a database system to keep track of daily repairs in preparation for the major repair does not come cheap.

In order to understand the technical skill of the maintenance company, it would be useful to find out whether they have large-scale repair contracts or not. Unlike regular condos, the repair of high-rise condos is more expansive and larger scaled, thus requires some qualified engineers including senior registered architects. These days, the biggest differentiation factor of the maintenance companies is nothing but their technical skills. Another factor would be their price negotiation skill with the affiliate companies.

According to the report published by Ministry of Land, Infrastructure, Transport and Tourism in 2013, average monthly repair fund payment is 206 yen/m^2 for high-rise condos with 20 or more floors. However, most of the condos above average turned out to be high-grade condos in the central Tokyo area.

The Secrets Behind High-Rise Condos ▮ **143**

Chapter 11 管理会社を見極める

アフターフィードバックの重要性

管理会社は、PDCA（plan-do-check-act）サイクルの一環で、管理組合や住民から寄せられた様々な意見を事業主に対してフィードバックしています。

フィードバックされた内容は、事業主の設計仕様書などに反映されることになり、その内容は右図のように多岐にわたります。このフィードバックの内容の報告の仕方で、管理会社のレベルが見えてきます。

通常管理会社は、事業主に対し事細かに住民からのクレームの内容を報告しています。ポイントは、管理会社が主体となって、クレーム内容を的確に分析し、優先順位を意識して対応しているかどうかということです。

何よりも最優先すべきことは、住民の安全にかかわることです。端的な例としては、駐車場の入り口のシャッターが壊れた場合などです。タワーマンションの駐車場のシャッターは開閉の頻度が桁違いに多く、故障や破損事故が起こりやすいものです。しかし、これはセキュリティ上大きな問題となります。何週間もシャッターを開放したままでは、管理会社のバックアップ体制が問われるということです。

Importance of Post-Sales Feedback

As a part of PDCA (Plan-Do-Check-Act) cycle, the maintenance company feeds back various inputs from the owners' association and from the residents to the developer.

The inputs from the residents spreading across many areas will be reflected in the design specifications of the developer. You can find the quality of the maintenance company by the way they report the inputs.

They usually report all the claims from the residents in detail to the developer. The important thing to look at is whether the maintenance company takes the leading role in analyzing the claim contents and taking actions by prioritizing the issues.

Examining Maintenance Companies

Residents' security should come first. We can pick the garage doors as an example. The garage doors of a high-rise condo are prone to fail or break due to their frequent use. This could expose the residents to security risks if any garage door is left open for weeks without getting a repair. If this should happen, you need to question the risk mitigation system of the maintenance company.

● タワーマンションの管理チェックポイント
Sample of Feedback Items Regarding Maintenance

外装 Exterior
- 欄干廻りからの落雪 Falling snow and ice from parapets
- コーナー部落雷 Lightning strikes at corner areas
- パネルの反射 Reflection from panels
- 小庇からの落雪 Falling snow and ice from small eaves
- 外壁タイルの剥離 Peeling of exterior tiles
- 落雪による庇の損傷 Damage to eaves by falling snow and ice

外構 Landscape
- 早い成長 Rapid growth
- 土質 Soil property
- 日照不足 Insufficient sunlight
- 樹液等による汚れ Sap stains

● 管理業務関係でフィードバックされる主な項目例
Sample of Feedback Items Regarding Maintenance

（修繕工事）
修繕工事体制づくり
修繕積立金不足、特に発電機や大型設備機器の予算精度の向上
共用部家具什器備品の修理

（ペット）
ルールの周知と違反者への対応

（駐車場）
駐車台数の減少への対応
車体規格オーバーへの対応

（その他）
敷地周辺の違法駐車対策

（Repair）
Organization of repair work task force
Insufficient repair funds, particularly accurate cost estimates of generator and large equipment
Repair of furniture in common area

（Pets）
Effective notification of rules and violation handling

（Parking）
Planning for decreasing number of cars in future
Handing of oversized cars

（Misc）
Handling of illegally parked cars outside of premises

Chapter 12

施工ミスはなぜおきる？
What Causes Construction Mistakes

Chapter 12 ▎施工ミスはなぜおきる？

後を絶たない施工ミス

一般的には、設計図通りに施工されていない場合に「施工ミス」ということになりますが、躯体工事でミスが起こると、是正のために一度打設したコンクリートを壊したり、鉄筋を再度つなぎ合わせたりする必要が生じます。このとき、是正の方法が適切かどうかを第三者検査機関に確認してもらう作業が加わります。建築基準法は、建物を建築する際に守らないといけない基本的な法律であり、たとえ施工後でも違反が発見された場合は違反建築物となり、違反部分を是正しない限り使用が制限されたり除却になることもあります。しかし、入居後に杭など基礎部分に施工ミスが発見された場合は、現実的に調査や是正工事が困難になります。

杭などの場合は、不同沈下による建物の傾きとして現れますが、配管のため梁に穴を空けて鉄筋を切断した場合は、一本の梁の性能が数％低下するものの、建物全体への影響はほとんど現れません。しかし、2005年の姉歯事件以降、建築基準法12条3項の運用が厳格になり、施工段階での構造の変更がほとんどできなくなりました。それ以前は、12条3項で、建設工事中に発生していた是正工事などについて変更申請をしていました。

姉歯事件以後、設計図通りにつくるということが最優先されるようになったため、性能を確保する前提での設計者の判断による変更が難しくなってしまいました。

Never Ceasing Construction Mistakes

In general, construction mistakes happen when the building is constructed differently from the original drawing. If this happens during the framework construction, a third party inspection will become necessary to verify the correction scheme for destroying the placed concrete and reconnecting the reinforced steel. The Building Standards Act is the basic code to conform to when constructing a building, and the building becomes illegal when a violation is found even after the completion.

In such a case the use of the building may become limited, and in the worst case, the

What Causes Construction Mistakes

building becomes subject to removal unless violation is corrected. When a violation is found in the base construction work including piling after people moved in, it would become virtually impossible to run an investigation and to conduct a correction work.

Piling violation will appear as a building tilt from uneven settlement, but reinforced steel cut from a drilled hole in the beam for piping purpose only degrades the performance of that beam by a few percent and its impact does not show up in the overall performance calculation of the building. After the falsified structural calculations problem in 2005 (a.k.a. the Aneha incident), the application of Article 12 Paragraph 3 of the Building Standards Act became stricter and this made any structural changes in the construction phase virtually impossible. It used to be possible to apply for partial changes based on this Article 12 Paragraph 3 in order to conduct a correction work.

Some modifications by architect's judgement in order to secure the performance of the building became extremely difficult since construction in perfect accordance to the drawing became the first priority after the Aneha incident.

● 施工ミスへの対処　Handling of Construction Mistakes

宅建業法上
購入者に不利な情報として購入者全員に情報開示
Act on Real Estate Transactions demands information disclosure to all buyers

建築基準法に違反している部分は是正義務
Any violation of Building Standards Act needs to be rectified

第三者による是正方法の確認
Verification of rectification scheme by 3rd party

是正完了　Completion of rectification

工事再開　Resume construction

重要事項説明書に記載　Make report in disclosure statement

Chapter 12 施工ミスはなぜおきる?

品質向上を阻む建設業界の重層構造

建築の質を高めようということが「住生活基本法（平成18年）」（188ページの「建築を取り巻く様々な法律」を参照）の基本施策で、そこには耐震性の向上や長寿命化、省エネルギー化などが示されています。しかし一方で、右図に示すように、業界の重層構造の中では、末端に行けば行くほど仕様ダウン、コストダウンしようとする圧力が強まります。これは、消費税増税も重要な要素になっています。この重層構造が、建設業界を疲弊させている要因の一つといわれています。比較的中規模のマンションでも、協力会社（下請）を一覧にした施工体制台帳の一覧表は、A3サイズに収まらないことがあります。

Construction Industry's Multi-Layered Hierarchy Blocking Quality Improvements

In order to improve the quality of buildings, the basic measures of the Basic Act for Housing (2006) (see "Various Acts Around Buildings" on page188) indicate improvements of earthquake resistance, prolonged lifespan and energy saving. One the other hand, as illustrated in the right figure, the pressure for loosened specifications and cost reduction grows stronger as you go down the industrial hierarchy. Accumulation effect of increase in consumption tax is an important factor for this pressure as well. This layered hierarchy is said to one of the factors exhausting the construction industry. Even for mid-sized condos, the work ledger for the construction work listing all the subcontractors sometimes becomes too big to fit in a A3 size sheet.

What Causes Construction Mistakes

● 建設業界の重層構造　Construction Industry's Multi-Layered Hierarchy

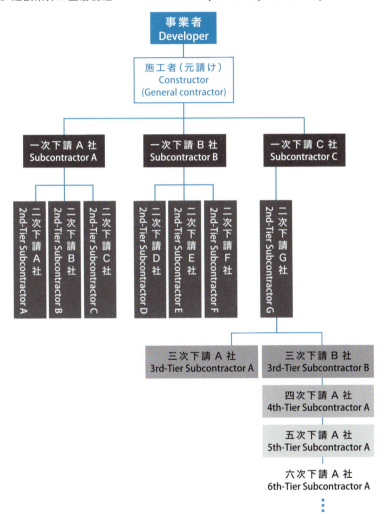

The Secrets Behind High-Rise Condos

Chapter 12 施工ミスはなぜおきる？

IT化の弊害

建設業界のIT化は、製造業とは異なり、製品が敷地毎の一品生産であるという性質上、効率化が難しいものとなっています。さらに、図面等の大容量のデータを扱う関係でネットワーク負荷が高く、一般の通信回線やクラウド等のデータ保管容量も、桁外れに大きくなります。

それでも最近は、大容量のストレージが安価で利用できるなど、建築に特化したベンダーの登場でIT化が一気に進むことに期待できます。

しかし一方で、利用する側の問題があります。今の時代、そもそも建築を志す学生の資質として、コンピュータが得意でないということがあるかもしれません。ソフトウェアを自分で開発し、HP作成、ネットを自在に操れる才能があれば、建築系よりも情報系に進むでしょう。

建設業界に就職すると、各企業にはすでにノウハウを蓄積したソフトウェアがあり、簡単な入力で工事費、工期がはじき出されます。しかも、すぐに会議資料になるようなもっともらしい出力が得られます。

いざ実際に土地取得から設計に入った途端、コンピュータでは分からなかった問題が発覚することがあります。多くの地中障害、複雑な地盤、周辺の道路状況がからみ、施工者からは工期の見直し要求が出ます。

しかし、どうしても年度末竣工引渡しをしなければならない物件があるのは事実です。開発担当者は、何が何でも年度末にできるという施工会社を探すことになります。結果、無理な工程を施工者に押しつけることになります。

今の建築業界のIT化は、あくまで、人間の考えることを忠実にシュミレーションするだけです。様々な条件は、新たに外部から条件を与えなければ、的確な結果は得られません。そのことを理解しないままIT化が進むと、現場との乖離がすすみ、施工不良が頻発することになりかねません。

What Causes Construction Mistakes

Issues Caused by IT Adoption

Unlike other manufacturing industries, IT adoption in the construction industry does not give much efficiency improvements as construction is a custom production and not a mass production. Also, handling of large data such as drawings will cause higher network load, and require order of magnitude greater data storage in the regular or the cloud environment.

However, construction-specific IT vendors started appearing in the market with their larger storage services at lower costs and we can expect an acceleration of adoption. There's however another problem on the user's side. Students pursuing architectural disciplines are not generally computer literate, and students with prolific IT knowledge such as software development, web page creation and networking skills are likely to go after IT-related careers.

Once found a job in the construction industry, a new grad will find every company has its own software build on its accumulated know-how that will instantly produce a nice-looking meeting-ready report of construction cost and period with simple inputs.

However, they may encounter unpredicted problems once the design starts after the land acquisition. With numerous ground obstacles, complex stratum and surrounding traffic situation, the construction company requests an extension of construction period.

But when the deadline for handover is set at the end of the fiscal year, the development manager will start looking for an alternative construction company that could complete the construction in time. As a result, they will impose an impossible schedule on the constructor.

The current IT offerings in the construction industry just perform faithful simulations of people's thinking. Unless proper conditions are fed, you cannot expect proper results. Driving IT adoption recklessly without understanding this fact can create even a bigger gap with constructors, and may result in more construction mistakes.

Chapter 12 施工ミスはなぜおきる？

杭設計の実態と課題

右のような支持地盤の上に立つ建築物は、杭の安全性について様々な検証を必要とします。建築基準法では、支持層への杭の到達とその貫入長さ、それに地震時の水平抵抗力の検討が求められ、支持層の安定性や、短い杭と長い杭の混在の検討などを行い、施工者にフィードバックします。また、工事が着工する前に、ボーリング調査に加えて、試掘をして支持層を確認します。

ここからが重要で、設計時の想定支持地盤と実際の支持地盤は通常多少異なります。販売時のパンフレットには、杭の施工方法や支持地盤までの深さ、杭のおおよその長さまで記載していますが、品確法では実際の施工の長さを記入した報告書を作成しますので、その数値の差が出ます。その数値差を気にして、なるべく設計図通りの長さで施工させようとする事業者の品質管理担当者がいることは事実です。このため事業者、設計者、施工者の三者の連携が重要になってきます。

Facts and Issues of Pile Design

You will need to examine many things concerning safety if a building stands on the supporting soil shown in the figure on the right page. The Building Standards Act requests the examination of the reach and the penetration lengths of the piles to the bearing ground as well as the lateral resistance of the piles. Then, you will also need to examine the stability of the bearing ground and the mixed use of short and long piles, and pass the examination results to the constructor. Before the construction starts, in order to check the bearing stratum, exploratory drilling survey will be conducted in addition to boring survey.

The important thing is that the actual bearing ground is usually located slightly different from the estimated one. In the sales collaterals, all the details including the piling method, the distance to the bearing ground, the rough lengths of the piles are stated, but you will see some differences with the actual lengths of the piles in the

What Causes Construction Mistakes

report requested by the Housing Quality Assurance Act. Some quality control manager of the developer will force the constructor to use the pile length described in the drawing so that there will be no length difference between the actual and the proejected piles. In order not to overlook such manipulation, it would be critical for all developer, architect and constructor to collaborate.

● 杭設計と実際の施工　Pile Design and Actual Piling

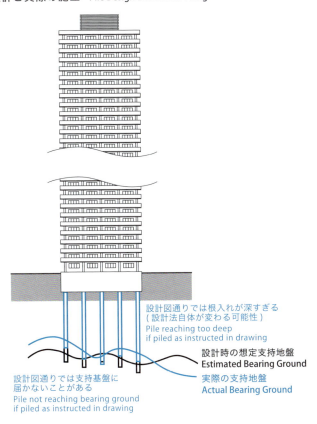

設計図通りでは根入れが深すぎる
(設計法自体が変わる可能性)
Pile reaching too deep
if piled as instructed in drawing

設計時の想定支持地盤
Estimated Bearing Ground

実際の支持地盤
Actual Bearing Ground

設計図通りでは支持基盤に
届かないことがある
Pile not reaching bearing ground
if piled as instructed in drawing

Chapter 13

タワーマンションの将来
Future of High-Rise Condos

Chapter 13 タワーマンションの将来

地震国日本に根付きつつある超高層マンション

東京だけでなく、全国で建設が続くタワーマンション。人間への心理的、生理的影響が懸念されつつも、今後のマンションの主流になりつつあります。

タワーマンションは、江戸時代の長屋の縦バージョン「縦長屋」といえるのではないかと思います。都市で人々が安全で快適に暮らすための、縦に連なった空間です。

しかし、各住戸は、分厚い床と遮音性を高めた壁でプライバシーが確保され、住民同士の交流ははなはだ難しい状況にあります。多くの都心のタワーマンションでは、区分所有者で住民3割、賃貸3割、オーナーチェンジ3割の住民構成となり、実際にコミュニティは成り立つのかという課題に直面しています。

このような状況で、住民の総意が必要な大規模改修にあたり、合意が不十分なまま構造的に不適切な改修工事が実施されて、建物の寿命を縮めることになったり、再度改修工事が必要となったりする例もあります。そのような場合、資産価値を大きく逸損することになりかねません。

Future of High-Rise Condos

High-Rise Condos Becoming Common in Quake-Plagued Japan

High-rise condos are being built not only in Tokyo but in many other places in Japan, and becoming the mainstream of condo buildings despite of some concerns about psychological and physiological effects on human.

I see high-rise condos as the vertical version of the terrace houses from the Edo period, the vertically connected spaces to provide safe and comfortable living in the city.

However, each unit is separated by thick floors and sound-insulating walls to secure privacy. This makes communication between residents very difficult. Also, in many high-rise condos in the city center, the percentages of owners, renters and renters with new owners are all 30 %, and their division of interests makes it hard to form a community of residents.

Such circumstances actually caused some cases of structurally improper repairs without proper consent and resulted in either shortening of building life or need for another repair. Such a case could lead to a serious loss of property value.

Chapter 13 ｜ タワーマンションの将来

今、タワーマンションに求められるもの

まず、事業者が、実際に100年以上の長期間にわたり建物が存在するということを真摯に受け止め、設計者、施工者と共に真に価値のある建築を目指すことが重要です。

現在の建築基準法の下では、施工ミスが、即、建替えになる可能性が高くなりました。業界をあげて、建築関連法規の根本的な見直しを含めた抜本的対策をしない限り、先細りする新築需要の中で、マンション事業は衰退していくことになることでしょう。

一方、すでに建てられた巨大マンション群が、そろそろ改修時期にさしかかっています。タワーマンションに特化した改修指針の必要性を感じています。新たな災害の時代に、大規模マンション群を街としてインフラをどのように維持管理するかも大きな課題です。巻末に改修ガイドラインの項目を列記してみました。

What to Require Now in High-Rise Condos

First of all, it is important for developers to understand the fact that the building will last over 100 years, and to work with architects and constructors to create architecture with true values.

Under the current Building Standards Act, it is highly likely that a construction mistake will directly lead to rebuilding. Unless the construction industry comes up with industry-wide drastic new measures, the condo business will be doomed to decline with the shrinking demands.

On the other hand, a group of existing giant condos are approaching the time of major repair. I strongly feel the need for the repair guidelines specialized for high-rise condos. Also, in this age of new disasters, it is a big challenge to address how to maintain the infrastructure of these giant condos as a town. There's a list of items to be included in such guidelines in the last section of this book.

Future of High-Rise Condos

● タワーマンションのコミュニティー　Community of High-Rise Condos

☞ 多様な価値観、生活環境の中での共同生活
Residents with different values and living environment
☞ 賃貸3割、平均年齢60歳以上
30 % renting and average age over 60

☞ コミュニティーの形成には協力的ではないが
災害時の相互扶助は求める傾向
Reluctant in forming community,
but opt for mutual help in case of disasters
☞ 資産価値の向上、生活環境の質的向上は求める傾向
Looking for increase in asset value and living standard

☞ 質の高い生活空間作りが求められている
High quality living space desired

Chapter 13 | タワーマンションの将来

空家問題

平成27年、「空家等対策の推進に関する特別措置法」が施行され、空き家対策が行われるようになってきましたが、今でも潜在的な空き家の数は、相当数に上ると言われています。

同様に、マンションでも空き家問題が表面化しつつあります。賃貸に出すには不便なマンションが、売るに売れない状況になるとますます話がこじれてきます。

賃貸で運用可能なタワーマンションは、これからも適正な修繕改修が行われると考えられますが、空き室が目立ち管理費の滞納が始まる前に、対策を打つ必要があります。

Vacancy Problem

In 2015, Act on Special Measures to Forward Municipalities' Moves for Vacant Premises went in effect to take necessary action on vacant houses, however, there are already considerable number of latent vacancies.

This problem is starting to surface for condos as well. We started seeing this vacancy problem in some condos not convenient for leasing. Things will get more difficult when you cannot sell them either.

We should be able to maintain and overhaul high-rise condos capable of leasing, but we'd still better to take some necessary measures before starting to see more vacancies and management fee delinquencies.

Future of High-Rise Condos

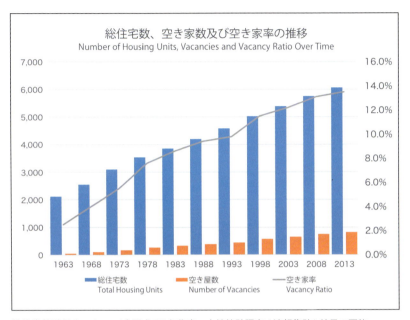

総務省統計局ホームページ 平成 25 年住宅・土地統計調査 (速報集計) 結果の要約
From Ministry of Internal Affairs and Communications Bureau of Statistics Web
http://www.stat.go.jp/data/jyutaku/2013/10_1.htm

Chapter 13　タワーマンションの将来

民泊問題

世界的規模で利用が進んでいる民泊紹介サイトにAirbnbがあります。タワーマンションの利便性を考え、今後うまく付き合っていく準備をする必要があると考えます。

投資、経済原理が優先される中で、世代交代しながら住み続けるためには、タワーマンションもホテルライクではなく、本当のホテルのようにセキュリティを確保し、さらに快適性を求めたリニューアルをほどこすべきではないかと考えます。そうして、更なる経済効果を発揮し、資産価値を高めていく方向も視野に入れておかなければなりません。さもなければ、日本だけがガラパゴス化してしまうことになりかねません。

B&B (Bed and Breakfast) Issues

Now that lodging services such as Airbnb are getting widely popular across the globe, we need to think about getting ready to take advantage of the convenient nature of high-rise condos.

The principles of investment and economy are the driving force of this movement. In order for our next generation to continue living in high-rise condos, we need to go ahead and renovate condos to provide security and comfort of real hotels to further promote economy effects and property value. Otherwise, only Japan may be left behind from the world.

Worawee Meepian / Shutterstock.com   Hung Chung Chih / Shutterstock.com

Chapter 13 タワーマンションの将来

建設業界のIT化

ゼネコン各社に見られる人手不足、建築資材の高騰、若手の建築業離れなど、建築は今や人気のない業界になっています。官民あげて職場環境づくりを目指していますが、なかなか前進していないのが実情です。

やはり、IT化を推進する以外に進むべき道はないというのが、私なりの結論です。実は、世の中には生産効率を高める様々な工夫をしているお手本の業界があります。それは車産業です。

工場内と野外の違いはありますが、品質管理の手法で取り入れられものは数多くあるはずです。特に、誰が、いつ、どんな作業を行ったかを管理することは、比較的容易にできる可能性があります。いわゆる、トレーサビリティです。

タワーマンションは、建築の中でも最も合理化されています。トレーサビリティのデータ化を始めることで更なる作業の効率化を、まずはタワーマンションで目指すということが現実的ではないかと考えます。

Promoting IT in Construction Industry

General contractors in Japan are hit by labor shortage, higher prices of building materials and less popularity of the industry among young people. They are working with the government to improve the working environment, but there's little progress made so far.

I've come to believe promoting IT is the only solution to this. We already have an excellent role model for production efficiency improvements, and that is the automotive industry.

Despite the difference in the indoors and outdoors construction, we should be able to learn a lot from them about the quality control methodology. In particular, it would be relative easy to track who did what when. This is called traceability.

Future of High-Rise Condos

Since construction of high-rise condos are most advanced in the industry as far as the rationalization is concerned, I feel it is very practical to start with recording the traceability data for high-rise condos to tackle the overall work efficiency improvements.

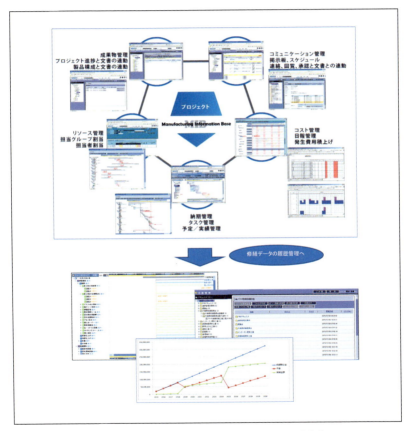

ITによる建築データ管理 Architectural Data Management Using IT Software
資料提供：株式会社シーイーシー (http://www.cec-ltd.co.jp/)

Chapter 13 | タワーマンションの将来

これからのタワーマンションに求められるもの

今、東京湾岸地域で起きているタワーマンションの開発には、都市としてのあり方を根本から変えてしまう可能性を感じます。

インフラの整備とともに夢でしかなかった未来都市ができつつあるのかもしれませんし、砂上の楼閣に過ぎないかもしれません。

しかし、その影響は、既に周辺地域にまで及んでいます。いわゆる裏銀座に次々と進出する新店舗もそのひとつで、ここは湾岸地域までタクシーで10分程度という利便性があり、夜遅くまで営業する店舗も増えてきています。

これまでの交通渋滞にも変化が見られます。以前のような首都高速道路の渋滞はなくなってきています。外環道三郷インターから市川ジャンクションが開通すると、都心の交通渋滞は、さらに緩和されることが期待されています。やがて、タワーマンションが東京という街全体に大きな影響力を持つことが予想されます。

集積する巨大マンション群に求められる安全レベルは、上部構造よりも基礎構造の安全性をよりいっそう高めることが重要ではないかと考えています。たとえば、四隅の杭は、他の杭の2倍の強度を持たせれば、万が一巨大地震がきて一本の杭が破壊しても、建物への影響は最小限にとどまるはずです。

What to Require in Future High-Rise Condos

In the current developments of high-rise condos in the Tokyo Bay area, I sense a possibility of changing the way a city operates.

They could be building a future city of dream with enriched infrastructure. Or those buildings could turn out to be just another castles in the air.

However, the impact of these developments is already propagating to the neighboring areas. New shops keep on opening in the back street area of Ginza. Taking location advantage of being only 10 minutes away from the bay area on a cab, many shops are open until late at night.

Future of High-Rise Condos

The traffic jam situation is changing, too. There's no more traffic jams on Metropolitan Expressway as seen before. The traffic situation in the city center is expected to improve further when they open the Ichikawa junction section from Misato interchange of Tokyo-Gaikan Expressway.

We foresee such effects of high-rise condos will spread all over Tokyo in the long run.

For the safety level required for densely populated giant condos, I feel it would be important to heighten the security more in the base structure than in the upper structure. For example, doubling the strength of the piles in four corners would minimize the damage to the building from a loss of one pile in a giant earthquake.

Chapter

14

知っておきたい建築の知識
Useful Information on Architecture

Chapter 14 知っておきたい建築の知識

新耐震設計法

昭和56年、それまでの地震時の強度を確保する設計法から、地震時のエネルギーを建物で吸収するという新しい考え方が導入されました。これにより、建物の変形能力や倒壊する形（崩壊モード）が耐震設計に反映されるようになりました。阪神淡路大震災では、新耐震設計以前と以後の建物では、明確に被害レベルが違っています。また、東日本大震災では「姉歯物件」に被害はなかったという話を聞きますが、震度5では、終局耐力に達していませんので、当然と言えばそれまでです。姉歯事件で問題となったのは、この終局耐力です。

Revised Seismic Design Method

A new idea of absorbing earthquake energy in the building structure instead of securing the strength against earthquakes was introduced in 1981. With this idea, deformation capacity of the building and the way the building collapses (called collapse mode) are taken into account in earthquake resistant designs. In the Great Hanshin-Awaji Earthquake, we saw a big difference in the damage level of the buildings built before and after this revised seismic design method. Some people say there was no damage in the buildings with the Aneha forged specifications in the Great East Japan Earthquake. But this is only because the intensity level of 5 was not big enough for the buildings to reach their ultimate strength. The Aneha Incident was all about this ultimate strength.

Useful Information on Architecture

阪神・淡路大震災による建築物等に係る被害

・阪神・淡路大震災における状況

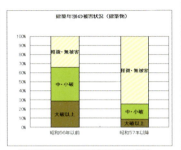

→ 死者数の大部分が建物等の倒壊が原因
→ 現在の耐震基準を満たさない昭和56年以前の建物に被害が集中

Document on Damages Caused by Hanshin-Awaji Earthquake Prepared by Ministry of Land, Infrastructure, Transport and Tourism (available in Japanese Only)

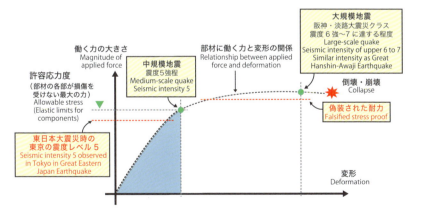

The Secrets Behind High-Rise Condos | 173

Chapter 14 | 知っておきたい建築の知識

長周期地震動

長周期地震動は、1985年のメキシコシティーでの地震被害から研究されるようになりました。そして、2003年9月の十勝沖地震での震央から250km離れた苫小牧の石油タンクの火災や、2007年7月の新潟県中越沖地震の際、新宿の超高層ビル群や丸の内のビル群が数分以上大きく揺れ動いたことから注目されるようになりました。2011年3月の東日本大震災でも、首都圏や大阪湾岸の超高層建築物が長時間揺れ続けました。今では、気象庁から長周期地震動階級が出されています。長周期地震動の本当の怖さは、その波、いわゆる波動エネルギーの持つ大きさです。周期の長い波は、減衰しにくく遠くまで伝わります。また、振動を減衰させる機構が弱いと、いつまでも揺れ続け損傷が拡大します。

Long-Period Earthquake Ground Motion

Extensive study started after the 1985 Mexico City Earthquake and the words "long-period earthquake" started receiving public attention when the Tokachi-oki Earthquake in September of 2003 caused a gasoline tank fire in Tomakomai 250 km away from the epicenter the and the Niigataken Chuetsu-oki Earthquake in July of 2007 shook high-rise buildings in Shinjuku and Marunouchi areas of Tokyo. Also, the Great East Japan Earthquake shook ultra-high-rise buildings in the Metropolitan Tokyo and Osaka bay areas for a long period of time. These days, Japan Meteorological Agency announces long-period earthquake ground motion intensity.

The real impact of long-period earthquake ground motion is in the magnitude of wave energy. Waves with long period tends to propagate a long distance and damage will become bigger if the damping mechanism is poor and the shake lasts for a long time.

Useful Information on Architecture

遠くまで伝搬する長周期地震動
Long-Period Earthquake Gound Motion Traveling Long Distance

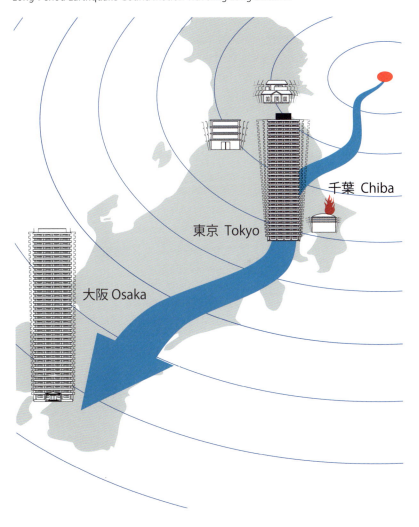

Chapter 14 知っておきたい建築の知識

Is 値 0.6 の意味

Is値とは、耐震指標（Seismic Index of Structure）のことで、「建築物の耐震改修の促進に関する法律」（平成７年12月施行）の中で、新耐震設計法とほぼ同等の震度6強程度の耐震性を有する値として、0.6という数字が示されています。
Is値 ≧ 0.6で表される安全性とは、「地震の震動及び衝撃に対し倒壊、又は崩壊する危険性が低い」と評価されるレベルです。

Meaning of Is Value 0.6

The seismic resistant performance of the building is judged from the Is (Seismic Index of Structure) value, and in the Act for Promotion of Renovation for Earthquake-Resistant Structures of Buildings (taken effect in January 1995), the value of 0.6 is considered to be approximately at the same safety level as described in the New Seismic Design Method.

The risk of collapse from the seismic motion and the impact of an earthquake is considered low when Is value is equal to or larger than 0.6.

Useful Information on Architecture

地震被害を受けた建物の Is 値分布 Is Value Distribution for Quake Damaged Buildings

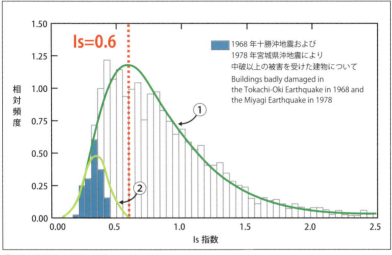

①：被害地震を未経験の建物の Is 値の分布
②：1968 年十勝沖地震及び1978年宮城県沖地震で中破以上の被害を受けた建物群の Is 値分布
　　(Is 値が 0.6 以上の場合は、中破以上の被害を受けていない)

①: Is value distribution of unharmed buildings
②: Is value distribution of buildings badly damaged in the Tokachi-Oki Earthquake in 1968 and the Miyagi Earthquake in 1978
　　(No serious damage was reported for buildings with 0.6 or better Is value)

中埜良昭、岡田恒男 (東京大学生産技術研究所): 信頼性理論による鉄筋コンクリート造建築物の
耐震安全性に関する研究 , 日本建築学会構造系論文報告集第 406 号 pp. 37-43, 1989 年 12 月
Reliability Analysis on Seismic Capacity of Existing Reinforced Concrete Buildings in Japan by Yoshiaki Nakano and Tsuneo Okada, Institute of Industrial Science, University of Tokyo

Chapter 14 知っておきたい建築の知識

地域係数 Z とは

地域係数 Z は、1952年（昭和27年）7月25日の「建設省告示第1074号」で定められたもので、河角廣東京大学地震研究所長が日本建築学会の機関誌『建築雑誌』(1951年4月20日号)で発表された、いわゆる「河角マップ」がもとになっています。

「地震力」＝「地震地域係数 Z」×「標準地震力」

日本全国の過去の地震の記録や書物をもとに算出した地震加速度により係数を定めたものです。東京では1.0、九州や北海道地方などは0.9や0.8の低減係数となり、静岡は条例で1.2とされています。地域係数Zの採用の経緯は専門書にゆずりますが、今問題となっているのは、Zが導入された昭和27年と現在では、地殻の活動状況が大きく異なっている点です。今や1,000年に一度の規模の地震が日本列島を襲っています。今年も政府の地震調査研究推進本部地震調査委員会は、「全国地震動予測地図」を発表しています。やがて、国土交通省告示に反映されることとなりますが、そもそも建築基準法は最低基準を示すものですから、実際に地震被害が起きてから係数が上げられるという結果となってしまいます。

Seismic Zoning Coefficient Z

Seismic coefficient Z was defined in the Ministry of Construction Notification No. 1458 promulgated on July 25, 1952 and was based on the "Kawasumi map" by Hiroshi Kawasumi, the then director of the Earthquake Research Institute of the University of Tokyo, originally published in the April 20, 1951 issue of Architectural Institute of Japan's "Journal of Architecture and Building Science."

Seismic force = Seismic zoning coefficient Z X Standard seismic force

This coefficient values are determined by seismic acceleration figures derived from past earthquake records and books all over Japan. The values are 1.0 for Tokyo, lower numbers of 0.8 and 0.9 for the Kyushu and Hokkaido areas, and 1.2 for Shizuoka by

Useful Information on Architecture

some regulations. We will not go into detail about the adoption background of this zoning coefficient Z, but would like to point out the big difference in diastrophism between now and 1952 when Z was introduced. Now earthquakes with once-in-thousand-year intensity are hitting the Japanese Archipelago. The Earthquake Research Committee of the Headquarters for Earthquake Research Promotion released the National Seismic Hazard Maps for Japan and this will be eventually reflected in the notification from the Ministry of Construction. Since the Building Standards Act is about securing the minimum standards, and therefore, the coefficient values will not be raised until quake disasters take place.

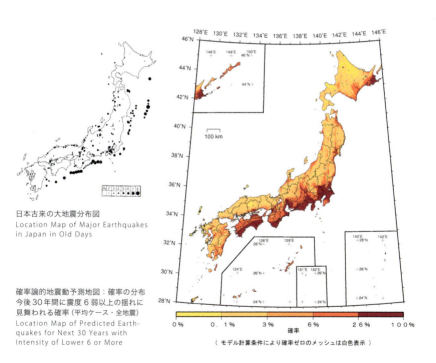

日本古来の大地震分布図
Location Map of Major Earthquakes in Japan in Old Days

確率論的地震動予測地図：確率の分布
今後30年間に震度6弱以上の揺れに
見舞われる確率（平均ケース・全地震）
Location Map of Predicted Earthquakes for Next 30 Years with Intensity of Lower 6 or More

Chapter 14 知っておきたい建築の知識

日本の活断層

原子力発電所の再稼働で話題となっている活断層ですが、その定義は意外と明確になっていません。国土地理院が刊行している活断層図では、地表に証拠を残すものと記されています。日本国中活断層が至る所にあります。逆に、この地殻変動が、日本の美しい山並みや海岸線を形作っているともいえます。問題となるのは、過去に大きな地震を引き起こしているかどうかで、活断層の地層の中にその痕跡が見つかることがあります。それは、「破砕帯」と呼ばれ、断層内の岩石が粉々に砕けている層のことです。

防災科学研究所により、活断層のABCが規定されていますが、あくまで地表に現れているものだけで、東京や大阪などの大都市の湾岸地域では、断層を形成する地層の上に数十メートルの柔らかい沖積層と呼ばれる地層が堆積しているため、見ることはできません。現在活断層は様々な方法で調査が進められていますが、どの活断層が動くかの予測は、まだまだ先のことになりそうです。

Active Faults in Japan

Active faults are drawing attention as the nuclear power plants resume operation. However, their definition is rather vague as even Geospatial Information Authority of Japan notes that their maps of active faults only cover the ones with surface traces. Still you could see active faults all over in Japan, and you could say the diastrophism caused by these faults has shaped the beautiful mountains and shorelines of Japan.

It is critical to learn whether the fault you are looking at caused major earthquakes in the past. You may be able to find the trace as crush zone in the stratum of the fault. Crush zone is a stratum in the fault that consists of crushed rocks.

Based on the average slip rate of the fault, National Research Institute for Earth Science and Disaster Prevention (NIED) categorize them into classes A, B and C where A represents largest. These faults are limited to the ones that can be observed

Useful Information on Architecture

from the surface. In the bay areas of big cities like Tokyo and Osaka, the strata forming faults are covered with another several-ten-meter-thick soft strata called alluvia and cannot be observed from the surface. Studies on active faults are in progress with various approaches, but it will be a while before we can predict their actual movement.

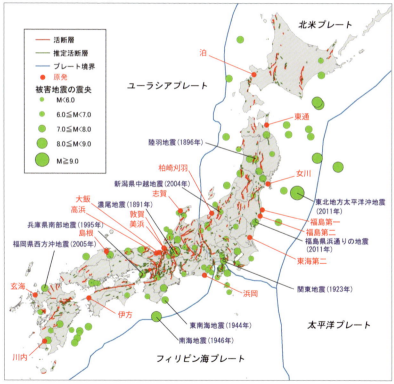

明治5(1872)年−平成23(2011)年に発生した主な被害地震の震央と陸域の活断層
(被害地震の震央は国立天文台編(2012)、活断層は中田・今泉(2002)から引用)
Epicenters of Major Earthquakes That Took Place Between 1872 and 2011 and Active Faults Observed on Lands
国土交通省 国土地理院「都市圏活断層図 利用の手引」より

Chapter 14 知っておきたい建築の知識

地盤の液状化現象

1964年6月16日に発生した新潟地震の際、信濃川河畔一帯で発生したことから広く知られるようになり、それ以降、地盤の液状化の研究は盛んに行われてきました。液状化現象は、もともと河川敷や三角州など水分を多く含んだ砂質地盤で発生しやすいと考えられていましたが、最近では、東京、千葉などの埋め立て地の多くで発生しています。

全国の液状化ハザードマップでおおよその地域が把握できます。

Soil Liquefaction

This phenomenon became well known and various studies became active after the Niigata Earthquake induced this in the riverside area of the Shinano River on June 16, 1964. Soil liquefaction was considered to take place in watery sand grounds such as waterbeds and deltas, but recently, we started seeing this in the landfill areas of Tokyo and Chiba as well.

You can find the potential hazard areas in the liquefaction hazard maps.

Useful Information on Architecture

新潟沖地震による液状化で倒れたアパート、その後起こして再利用
Apartment buildings tumbled by soil liquefaction of Niigata-Oki Earthquake. Raised for reuse later

液状化によりむきだしになったマンホール
Exposed sewer by soil liquefaction

Chapter 14 | 知っておきたい建築の知識

PML (Provable Maximum Loss) 値とは？

PMLとは予想最大損失率のことで、一般にはあまり知られていない値ですが、もともとはアメリカで生まれた概念で、火災保険料などを算定する指標とされ、1980年代から地震に対しても適応するようになりました。これは、475年に一度起こる規模の最大の地震が起きたとき、建物が被る損害の補修費用の新築費用に対する割合を示したものです。日本でも不動産の証券化や不動産投資の将来収益予測に用いられ、投資基準の指標となっています。

具体例をあげると、現時点で新築すると100億円かかる建物が再現期間475年の大地震を受けたときに補修する費用が13億円かかるとすると、PML値は13/100で13%となります。修復不能で建替えの場合には100%ということになります。

ただし、各社独自の算出方法が採用されているため、数値にばらつきがあるなどといった問題点が指摘されています。

PML (Provable Maximum Loss) Value

Though not well known, this concept was born in the US to calculate the fire insurance premium. In the 1980s, they started adopting this for earthquakes as well to indicate the ratio of repair cost to build cost of the building when hit by a giant earthquake that only happens once in 475 years. In Japan, this becomes an index for investment criteria and used for real estate securitization and expected return of real estate investments.

If a building that costs 10 billion yen to build new encounters a huge earthquake of 475-year return period and requires repair cost of 1.3 billion, PML value will be 13/100 = 13%. In the unrepairable case, this figure would be, of course, 100%.

Some people point out an inconsistency issue between companies as calculation method of PML is somewhat company dependent.

Useful Information on Architecture

性能マトリクスの例　Performance Matrix Sample

地震レベル	性能レベル			
	全機能維持	機能維持	人命保護	崩壊寸前
30年超過確率 50%（再現期間 43年）	○			
50年超過確率 50%（再現期間 72年）	○	○		
50年超過確率 10%（再現期間 475年）	○	○	○	
50年超過確率 5%（再現期間 970年）	○	○	○	○

（基本性能目標 — diagonal line through 43年/全機能維持 → 72年/機能維持 → 475年/人命保護 → 970年/崩壊寸前）

Earthquake Design Level (Return Period)	Earthquake Performance Level			
	Fully Operational	Operational	Life Safe	Near Collapse
Frequent (43 year)	○	×	×	×
Occasional (72 year)	□	○	×	×
Rare (475 year)	☆	□	○	×
Very Rare (970 year)		☆	□	○

× : Unacceptable Performance (for New Construction)　　○ : Basic Objective
□ : Essential/Hazardous Objective　　☆ : Safety Critical Objective

From the Structural Engineers Association of California Vision 2000 document

Chapter 14 | 知っておきたい建築の知識

見たことありますか？ 東京都耐震マーク

東京都の場合、耐震改修済の建物には、「耐震マーク」が無償で交付されます。ただし、耐震性や耐久性を保証するものではなく、あくまで、新耐震設計法に適合していることや、耐震改修法のIs値0.6以上が確保できているという意味です。

Have You Seen the Tokyo Earthquake Resistance Sticker?

Tokyo Metropolitan Government issues earthquake resistance stickers at no cost if the buildings conforms to the new earthquake resistance measures. This, however, only indicates conformance to the new measures and a better-than 0.6 Is value, and does not guarantee actual resistance or durability.

Useful Information on Architecture

3. 課題に対する現行の取組み

② 耐震性があるという認識など、耐震化が不要と考えている

【現行の取組み】
- 耐震改修促進法に基づき、多数の者が利用する建築物などに対して、耐震診断・耐震改修の努力義務を課すとともに、所管行政庁による指導・助言・指示等を実施している。
- 既存建築物耐震診断・改修等推進全国ネットワーク委員会や東京都、横浜市において、耐震性のある建築物に表示できる制度を創設している。

国土交通省「住宅・建築物の耐震化と現状の課題について」

Document on Earthquake Resistance Challenges Prepared by Ministry of Land, Infrastructure, Transport and Tourism (available in Japanese Only)

Chapter 14 知っておきたい建築の知識

建築を取り巻く様々な法律

建築基準法、建築士法、建設業法、住宅の品質確保の促進等に関する法律（品確法）、住生活基本法、都市計画法、消防法、水道法、下水道法、浄化槽法、バリアフリー法、高齢者、身障者等の移動等の円滑化の促進に関する法律、耐震改修促進法、文化財保護法、景観法、長期優良住宅の普及の促進に関する法律、区分所有法、宅地建物取引業法（宅建業法）など、建築には他にも多くの関係法令があります。

特に建築基準法は、その目的に、「国民の生命、健康及び財産の保護」がうたわれています。

Various Acts Around Buildings

Such acts include Building Standards Act, Act on Architects and Building Engineers, Construction Business Act, Housing Quality Assurance Act, Basic Act for Housing, City Planning Act, Fire Service Act, Water Supply Act, Sewerage Service Act, Sewage system Act, Barrier-Free Act, Act on Promotion of Smooth Transfer for Elderly Persons and Physically Disabled People in Public Transportation Use, Act for Promotion of Renovation for Earthquake-Resistant Structures of Buildings, Act on Protection of Cultural Properties, Landscape Act, Act on Promotion of Long-Term High-Quality Housing, Unit Ownership Act, and Act on Real Estate Transactions. There are also related laws about architecture.

Particularly, the Building Standards Act claims protection of Japanese people's lives, health and property as its objective

Useful Information on Architecture

	制定	（目的）第一条 抜粋
建築基準法	昭和25年	この法律は、建築物の敷地、構造、設備及び用途に関する最低の基準を定めて、国民の生命、健康及び財産の保護を図り、もって公共の福祉の増進に資することを目的とする。
建築士法	昭和25年	この法律は、建築物の設計、工事監理等を行う技術者の資格を定めて、その業務の適正をはかり、もって建築物の質の向上に寄与させることを目的とする。
建設業法	昭和24年	この法律は、建設業を営む者の資質の向上、建設工事の請負契約の適正化等を図ることによって、建設工事の適正な施工を確保し、発注者を保護するとともに、建設業の健全な発達を促進し、もって公共の福祉の増進に寄与することを目的とする。
住宅の品質確保の促進等に関する法律（品確法）	平成11年	この法律は、住宅の性能に関する表示基準及びこれに基づく評価の制度を設け、住宅に係る紛争の処理体制を整備するとともに、新築住宅の請負契約又は売買契約における瑕疵担保責任について特別の定めをすることにより、住宅の品質確保の促進、住宅購入者等の利益の保護及び住宅に係る紛争の迅速かつ適正な解決を図り、もって国民生活の安定向上と国民経済の健全な発展に寄与することを目的とする。
住生活基本法	平成18年	この法律は、住生活の安定の確保及び向上の促進に関する施策について、基本理念を定め、並びに国及び地方公共団体並びに住宅関連事業者の責務を明らかにするとともに、基本理念の実現を図るための基本的施策、住生活基本計画その他の基本となる事項を定めることにより、住生活の安定の確保及び向上の促進に関する施策を総合的かつ計画的に推進し、もって国民生活の安定向上と社会福祉の増進を図るとともに、国民経済の健全な発展に寄与することを目的とする。

Excerpts from Various Acts Stating Protection of Life and Quality of Buildings (in Japanese Only)

Chapter 14 知っておきたい建築の知識

区分所有法

昭和30年代に入り、主に都市部で中高層の複合用途ビルや分譲マンションの供給が行われるようになり、従来の民法の規定だけではその権利関係に対応することが困難な状況になってきたことから、昭和37年に区分所有法が制定されました。その後、分譲マンションの急増に伴い制度の不備が指摘されるようになり、改正が重ねられています。昨今では、建替え要件が全住戸の同意から4/5、3/4と引き下げられ、建替えの促進を図る方向の改正がなされています。

しかし現在、タワーマンションは、2,000戸を超える巨大なコミュニティになってきています。区分所有法を定めた昭和30年代の分譲マンションとは、全く異なるものであることは明らかです。建築基準法と共に、根本的な見直しが必要な時期にきているといわれているのはそのためです。

Building Unit Ownership Act

In late 1950s, with an introduction of mixed-use buildings and condos mainly in the city areas, the conventional civil law started to see some difficulties in handling relationship of rights and Act on Building Unit Ownership was enacted in 1962.

Between then and now, with the rapid increase of condos, it went through many amendments to rectify shortcomings. During the course, the requirement for rebuilding has been lowered from 100 % consent of all the units to 80%, then to 75 % in order to promote rebuilding.

These days, a high-rise condo forms a huge community of more than 2,000 units and turned into something completely different from the one in the 1960s when the Act on Building Unit Ownership was enacted. This is why the act along with Building Standards Act is said to be about time for complete revision.

Useful Information on Architecture

区分所有法の制定時の背景と考え方

『建物の区分所有等に関する法律の解説』(川島一郎 1962)、『コンメンタール マンション区分所有法』(稲本洋之助、鎌野邦樹 2004)より国土交通省作成

区分所有法立法以前(～昭和37年)

○ 建物の区分所有は、以前から旧民法第208条(建物等の共用部分は区分所有者の共有と推定、共用部分の修繕費等は各自の所有部分の価格割合で分担)により認められていたが、当時は高層住宅は少なく、あまり重要な機能を営んではいなかった。

区分所有法立法時(昭和37年)

○ しかし、昭和30年代後半になって、ビルディングの建築が盛んになり、建物を階層的に区分所有する事例が増えたが、当該民法の規定しかなかったことから、管理に支障が生ずる恐れがあり、適切な立法措置が望まれたのが背景。

○ 共用部分共有持分は専有部分と分離して処分することはできない旨規定したが、専有部分と敷地利用権の分離処分を禁止する規定は設けなかった。これは、常に一般の建物所有の場合との不均衡を招くことなく、土地所有権なり、敷地権一般の問題として考慮したため。

○ 管理者の選任、規約、集会の規定は任意的な制度として規定され、管理組合に関する規定は設けられなかった。

区分所有法改正時(昭和58年)

○ 専有部分と敷地利用権を一体とし、分離処分の禁止を規定。

○ 区分所有建物にあっては、その建物並びに敷地及び付属施設の管理を行うことを目的とする団体が区分所有者全体によって当然に構成されるものとみなし、そのような団体の存在を前提として、区分所有者は、集会を開き、規約を定め、管理者を置くことができる旨規定した。

国土交通省「マンション管理の現状等について」
Document on Background of Building Unit Ownership Act Prepared by Ministry of Land, Infrastructure, Transport and Tourism (available in Japanese Only)

Chapter 14 | 知っておきたい建築の知識

日本のリサイクル法

日本経済の発展に伴う大量の廃棄物の再利用を促進するため、1991年（平成3年）に「資源の有効な利用の促進に関する法律」が制定されています。以下のように対象種類毎に法律が定められています。

容器包装リサイクル法
瓶・缶・包装紙・ペットボトルなどの分別回収や再資源化を促進。
容器包装に係る分別収集及び再商品化の促進等に関する法律を参照。

家電リサイクル法
エアコン・洗濯機・冷蔵庫・テレビなどの家庭用の電気製品（使用済）について製造業者・輸入業者に回収と再利用を義務化。特定家庭用機器再商品化法を参照。

小型家電リサイクル法
使用済みの携帯電話・デジタルカメラなどの小型家電製品からレアメタルなどを取り出して再資源化を促進。
使用済小型電子機器等の再資源化の促進に関する法律を参照。

建設リサイクル法
コンクリートや木材の再資源化を促進。
建設工事に係る資材の再資源化等に関する法律を参照。

食品リサイクル法
食品に関する製造業者・加工業者・販売業者に食品のゴミの再資源化を促進。
食品循環資源の再生利用等の促進に関する法律を参照。

自動車リサイクル法
使用済自動車の解体時に部品などについて製造業者・輸入業者に回収処理を義務化。
使用済自動車の再資源化等に関する法律を参照。

パソコンリサイクル法
使用済パーソナルコンピュータの回収と再資源化を図る。
資源の有効な利用の促進に関する法律を参照。

Useful Information on Architecture

Recycling Regulations in Japan

In order to promote recycling of massive waste increased with the expansion of Japanese economy, Law for Promotion of Effective Utilization of Resources was enacted in 1991. It consists of individual laws for various objects.

Containers and Packaging Recycling Law

To promote sorted collection and recycling of glass bottles, cans, containers, packaging wastes and PET bottles. Refer to Act on the Promotion of Sorted Collection and Recycling of Containers and Packaging.

Home Appliance Recycling Law

To mandate manufacturers and importers to collect and recycle (used) home electrical appliances including air conditioners, washing machines, refrigerators and TV sets. Refer to Act on Recycling of Specified Kinds of Home Appliances.

Small Electrical Equipment Recycling Law

To promote recycling of rare metals used in small electrical equipment including used cell phones and digital camera. Refer to Act on Promotion of Recycling of Small Waste Electrical and Electronic Equipment.

Construction Material Recycling Law

To promote recycling of concrete and wood. Refer to Construction Material Recycling Act.

Food Recycling Law

To promote recycling of food waste by food manufacturers, processors and retailers. Refer to Act on Promotion of Recycling and Related Activities for Treatment of Cyclical Food Resources.

End-of-Life Vehicle Recycling Law

Mandate manufacturers and importers to collect scrap parts from used cars. Refer to Act on Recycling, etc. of End-of-Life Vehicles.

Personal Computer Recycling Law

To promote collection and recycling of used personal computers. Refer to Act on the Promotion of Effective Utilization of Resources.

Chapter 14 知っておきたい建築の知識

既存不適格建物とは

建築基準法が改正されると、それ以前の建物は、新しい基準を満たさない限り、既存不適格建物となります。

問題が発生するのが、増改修工事の際に用途変更等で確認申請が必要になる場合です。耐震補強工事など例外はありますが、原則として既存部分を現行法に適合するように改修する必要があります。

タワーマンションでは、様々な部分で高度な技術が使われているため、この改修を行うことはほとんど不可能なことが多く、住民の意見で必要のなくなった用途を別な用途で使いたいと考える際の大きな障壁となっています。

しかし、平成12年までに建築基準法第38条の国土交通省大臣の認定で建てられた建物は、既存不適格建物とされていましたが、平成27年に第38条が復活し容積率の緩和もありました。今後の弾力的な運用を期待したいところです。

Existing Non-Conforming Buildings

When the Building Standards Act is amended, an existing building will become non-conforming unless it satisfies the new criteria.

Problems happen when you are required to apply for building certification in the case of extension and repair. Except for seismic reinforcements, you are generally required to modify the existing parts of the building so that they conform to the current building code.

Improvements of high-rise condos are almost impossible due to the sophisticated technologies used in various parts of the building, and this fact is a big obstacle when the residents hope to use some parts of the building for other purposes.

The buildings built before 2000 with authorization from Minister of Land, Infrastructure and Transport based on the Building Standards Act Article 38 became non-conforming after Article 38 was removed in 2000. However, Article 38 was

Useful Information on Architecture

reinstated along with the relaxation of floor area ratio requirements in 2015. We hope dynamic utilization of these in the future.

違法建築物と既存不適格建築物　Illegal and existing non-conforming buildings

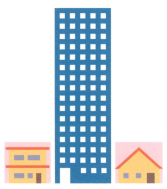

違法建築物（面積オーバー）
Illegal Buildings (Building-to-Land Ratio Violation)

既存不適格建築物（高さオーバー）
Existing Non-Conforming Building (Height)

Chapter 14 | 知っておきたい建築の知識

超高強度コンクリート

コンクリート強度といっても、圧縮、引張り、曲げ、せん断、支圧、疲労、鉄筋との付着強度がありますが、一般には、圧縮強度のことを指しています。鉄の引張り強度と比較をしたものが右図ですが、最近では鉄の強度の領域に迫ってきています。100Nを超える強度のコンクリートが超高強度コンクリートと呼ばれています。この技術が高さ200mを超えるタワーマンションを支えているのです。

Ultra-High-Strength Concrete

The strength of concrete is defined by various measures including compressive, tensile, bending, shear, bearing, fatigue and bond strengths, and compressive strength is most widely used. The right figure illustrates the strengths of various types of concrete against the tensile strength of iron, and as you could see, concrete is getting as strong as iron. Ultra-high-strength concrete has a strength over $100N/mm^2$ and is able to support high-rise condos over 200m in height.

Useful Information on Architecture

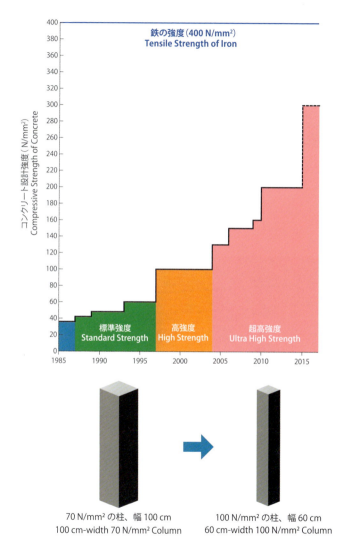

異なるコンクリート材による同強度の柱の幅比較
Width Comparison of Columns with Same Strength But Made with Different Concrete

The Secrets Behind High-Rise Condos

Chapter 14　知っておきたい建築の知識

シートフローリング

平成18年頃から急速に普及し、今では多くのタワーマンションで採用されている床材です。木板の表面にプリントされたオレフィンシートを貼り付けたもので、大日本印刷や凸版印刷など印刷メーカーのプリント技術の進歩に伴い、様々な模様が可能になったことと、表面のコーティング層が摩擦や傷に強く、仕上げ検査や内覧会での指摘が劇的に減少したため、今ではタワーマンションの床材の定番となっています。

Useful Information on Architecture

Sheet Flooring

It started getting widely used since 2006 and has become the standard flooring material in many high-rise condos. It is made by pasting a grain-printed olefin sheet on a wood plate. Various grain patterns became available with the advanced printing technologies developed by major printing companies such as DNP and Toppan, and number of complaints at both preliminary and final inspections significantly dropped thanks to friction and scratch resistant surface coating. Now, sheet flooring has become the new standard in high-rise condos.

Chapter 14 ▎知っておきたい建築の知識

ALCパネル

1920年代にスウェーデンで開発されて以来、ヨーロッパを中心に世界中で用いられ、日本では旭化成が1960年代から生産を始めた歴史のある材料です。タワーマンションでは、バルコニーの外壁や避難階段の区画壁の定番として使用されています。間仕切り壁の「石膏ボード」とあわせると、建築内装工事材料の大半を占めます。ALCパネルを風雨が直接当たる部分に用いているタワーマンションの場合、塗装自体は、施工にもよりますが、10年前後は問題ありません。しかし、防水シールは5年もすれば劣化が進み、そこからALCパネルに水分が浸透し、強度低下、塗装の劣化、苔の発生など、様々な劣化が進行します。そのため日頃のメンテナンスや入念な点検が欠かせません。定番ゆえに材料の特性を十分理解した上で、使用する必要があります。

外壁ALCパネルにタイル張りの仕様は、論外ですが、ごくたまに見かけます。
早急に専門家を入れて、今後起こりうる事態に備える必要があります。

ALC (Autoclaved Lightweight Concrete) Panels

Since its invention in 1920s in Sweden, ALC panels are in wide use all over the world particularly in Europe. In Japan, Asahi Kasei started the production in 1960s and established a long history already. They are the standard material in high-rise condos for exterior wall of balcony and section wall of emergency stairs. Together with plaster boards for room partitioning, they account for the vast majority of the internal work materials.

The durability varies depending on the construction quality, but ALC panel coating of high-rise condos exposed to rain and wind will be fine for the first ten years or so on average. However, water sealing starts to deteriorate after about five years and water will penetrate into the panels to cause various degradation including lower strength, weathered coating and moss formation. Thus, daily maintenance and

Useful Information on Architecture

thorough inspection will be mandatory. Also, ALC panels should be used properly by understanding the characteristics well.
Tiled exterior ALC panels are out of question, but used in some buildings. The residents of such buildings should consult an expert to take proper action against the situation to come.

ALC パネルを使った外壁
Exterior Walls Using ALC panels

Chapter 14 | 知っておきたい建築の知識

タワーマンションの工事工程の見方

タワーマンションの工程のポイントはいくつかあります。

1. 基礎工事

一日に数百立方メートルのコンクリートを打設することもあり、天候、特に集中豪雨などで打設日がずれると大幅な工程遅延につながります。杭工事を含めた地下部分の工事にどの程度の余裕があるかがポイントです。

2. 地上部

地上サイクル工程の着手日は厳守する必要があります。PC工場からの輸送、日々のコンクリート打設計画を当初の計画通り着実に進めるための大前提です。この日がずれ込むようだと工程回復の見込みは少なく、最上階付近の仕上げ工程や竣工検査工程、内覧会の実施日などに影響が出ます。

3. 設計時での工程短縮

設計段階であれば、タワークレーンの能力を上げることや、仮設計画を見直したり、逆打ち工法を採用するなど、打つ手はいくつかあります。しかし、逆打ち工法では、地上部と地下部で同時に工事が行われるので、事前の施工図の承認など施工者のみならず、監理者にも多くの負担がかかることになります。タワーマンションでは、最上階に近づくに従って、タワークレーンの揚重速度が工程に大きく影響します。

How to Read Construction Schedule of High-Rise Condos

There are several milestones in construction schedule of high-rise condos.

1. Foundation work

Since sometimes several hundred cubic meter of concrete is placed in a day, the weather, torrential downpours in particular, could significantly delay the overall construction schedule. You want to make sure they have some margin in the underground construction schedule including the time for piling to absorb such delay.

Useful Information on Architecture

2. Above ground construction

Start date for cyclic construction process above ground must not be delayed as that is the essential prerequisite for on-schedule transport of the PC parts from the factory and daily concrete placement. If the schedule slips, there's little hope for recovery and all the dates for finishing of top floors, completion inspection and preliminary inspection will be pushed out.

3. Shortening construction period in design phase

While in design phase, you can do several things to make up for the delay including the use of high performance tower crane, reevaluation of temporary work plan, and the use of inverted construction. However, inverted construction will have a big impact on both constructor and administrator because of simultaneous works above ground and under and the need for preapproval of working drawings. In higher stories, the lifting speed of tower cranes will have a big impact on the schedule.

逆打ち工法（地下部分） Inverted Construction

タワークレーン Tower Crane

Chapter 14　知っておきたい建築の知識

大規模修繕工事の実際

最初の工程表の精査が、その後の管理組合総会や理事会の決議に大きく影響を与えます。コンサルタントや設計事務所を選定する場合、空調機器等の設備機器との改修手順や、工事内容の調整が具体的なイメージとして、プレゼンテーションされているかどうかが重要です。

施工者を決める手順は、設計監理か設計施工かというテーマで本文中にも触れましたが、大規模修繕工事でもやはり、担当者の力量とそのバックアップ体制ができているかを見極めることが重要です。

Realities of Large-Scale Repair

Close examination of the initial repair schedule would have a big impact on the decisions from the owners' maintenance association meeting and from the board of directors. When choosing a consultant or a design office, it is important to make sure they present the repair procedure of the equipment including air conditioners as well as the work contents arrangements in a concrete fashion.

The choice of constructor is covered in the "Design Administration Vs. Design and Construction" section, but it is important to evaluate their capabilities and backup system.

Useful Information on Architecture

大規模修繕工事の流れ Flow diagram of large-scale repair

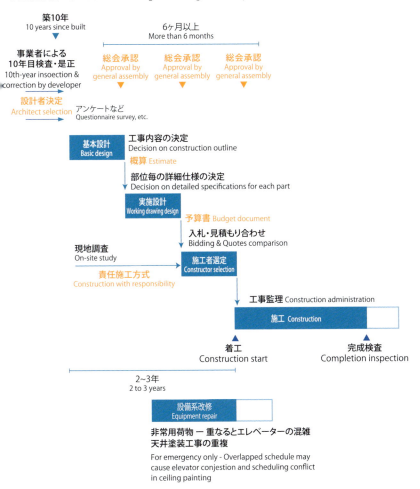

Chapter 14 | 知っておきたい建築の知識

サステナブル建築

サステナブルとは、「持続可能な」と訳されています。建築でのサステナブルとは一般的に、以下のようにとらえられています。

1. 建築のライフサイクルを通じての省エネルギー・省資源・リサイクル・有害物質排出抑制をする。
2. 地域の気候、伝統、文化および周辺環境と調和する。
3. 将来にわたって人間の生活の質を適度に維持あるいは向上させていくことができる。

狭い意味では、環境負荷を低減する建築をサステナブル建築と呼ぶ場合がありますが、現在、「サステナブル建築物等先導事業（省 CO_2 先導型）」などで積極的に推進されています。

タワーマンションが「サステナブル建築」かどうかは大いに議論の余地はありますが、少なくとも建設時よりも維持管理コストを低減するという課題を人知によって克服する必要があります。

Sustainable Architecture

The requirements for sustainable architecture are considered as follows:

1. Will reduce energy and resource consumption, promote recycling and suppress hazardous materials emission throughout architecture's lifecycle
2. Will adjust to climate, tradition, culture and environment of the area
3. Will be able to properly maintain or improve quality of life for years to come

In the narrow sense, a building that reduce environmental load is called sustainable architecture. Currently, this idea is heavily promoted by initiatives such as Pilot Business Project for Sustainable Architecture (CO_2 Reduction Pilot Project).

The question whether high-rise condos are sustainable is subject to an open discussion, but at least, we will have to give our best to reduce maintenance costs than that at the construction completion.

Useful Information on Architecture

植物を多用したタワーマンション　Green High-Rise Condos

Bosco Verticale, Milan, Italy

Eugenio Marongiu / Shutterstock.com

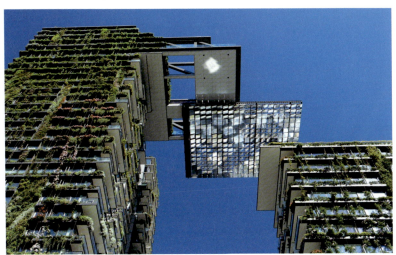

Blancas One Central Park, Sydney, Australia

SAKARET / Shutterstock.com

Chapter 14 ┃ 知っておきたい建築の知識

超高層マンション改修ガイドライン

全国分譲マンションの数は、613万戸を超え今も毎年10万戸以上増え続けています。一方で、昭和56年以前の耐震基準で建てられた、いわゆる旧耐震の建物は100万戸を超え、耐震改修が求められています。平成9年の規制緩和以降に急増した大規模タワーマンションも大規模修繕工事の時期にきています。

タワーマンションに限れば、竣工後10～15年目に迎える1回目の大規模修繕工事は、積立金もあり、順調に進んでいるように見えます。しかし、超高層鉄筋コンクリート建築にほとんど知識のないコンサル会社や施工会社が、低層マンションの外壁ひび割れを直すのと同じ感覚で施工している例も少なくありません。湾岸地域の建物は、海からの潮風で、コンクリートの中性化の進行が早まります。特に、外壁のひび割れから急速な劣化が見られることがあるので、専門家の的確な判断が求められますが、理事会や総会のスケジュールでそれらの検討材料について具体的な決定が先延ばしになったりすれば後々大きな代償を払うことになりかねません。研究機関などによる超高層マンションに特化した改修ガイドライン作成が待たれます。超高層鉄筋コンクリート構造の建築の改修に携わる上での最低限必要と思われる知識を元に列記してみました。改修設計コンサルタントには必ず押さえてほしい内容です。

Ultra-High-Rise Condos Renovation Guidelines

Number of condo units in Japan exceeds 6.13 million and continues to grow more than one hundred thousand every year. On the other hand, more than one million buildings built conforming to the old (pre-1981) earthquake resistance regulations are subject to seismic reinforcement. Also, many large-scale high-rise condos built after the 1997 deregulation are about to go through major repair.

As far as the high-rise condos are concerned, you may not see a problem in the first major repair with sufficient reserve fund. However, there are cases where unexperienced and ignorant consulting and construction firms that have little

Useful Information on Architecture

knowledge on ultra-high-rise reinforced concrete buildings doing repair works as if they are fixing cracks of exterior walls of low-rise condos. Concrete of buildings in bay areas will rapidly carbonate by sea wind. Particularly as cracks of exterior walls may accelerate the deterioration, inputs from expertise are desirable. You may end up paying a big price if the decision on these issues from the owners' meeting and the board of directors is delayed because of schedule conflicts. Repair guidelines specific to high-rise condos from some research institute would be very helpful.

The table on this page is the minimum list of items necessary for repairing ultra-high-rise reinforced concrete buildings. Repair consultants should go through these items without fail.

1. 基本構造の確認 (Check basic structure)	大臣認定書の確認 旧 38 条認定かどうか 使用材料の確認 避難関連 (Check Minister Certification to find whether old Building Standards Act Article 38 conformance or not. Also check for materials used and evacuation process)
2. 現在の振動性状の確認 (Check for current vibration property)	振動性状の確認 (Check vibration property)
3. 耐震、免震、制震 (Seismic resistance, vibration control and seismic isolation)	常時微動測定からの推定 (Estimate from microtremor measurements)
4. 施工記録 (Construction records)	竣工図書などとの照合・確認 (Check and confirm completion documents) 新技術の開発・導入 タイル外壁の将来 (Development and adoption of new technologies, future plan for tile exterior walls)
5. 外壁の改修設計 (Repair design of exterior walls)	乾式 (ALC 等) 壁のロッキングシステムなどが機能しているか確認 (Check correct operation of locking system of dry walls)
6. 将来計画 (Future plan)	2 回目以降の大規模修繕工事を想定した仮設計画 (Temporary plan for second and sunsequent major repair works) 建物寿命を考慮した改修計画の実施 (Execution of building-lifespan-aware repair plan) 長期修繕計画 100 年三世代 (Long-term repair plan for 100 years and three generations)
7. その他 (Miscellany)	PC 化と工法の検証 コンクリート強度はどこまで強くなるか (Verify PC adoption and construction method and future concrete strength improvements) 設計上の留意点 アウトフレーム、パネルゾーンなど (Important notes on outframing, panel zones, etc.)

Chapter 14 知っておきたい建築の知識

敷地の歴史をひもとく

設計者は大規模な開発になればなるほど、その敷地の歴史や成り立ちを入念に調べます。首都圏、特に東京駅周辺は、江戸時代からの古地図があります。書店でも販売されていますが、その土地の成り立ちを知るには欠かせない情報です。溜池などの池を埋め立ててできた土地、旧江戸城の外堀を埋め立ててできた土地では、支持層が平坦ではなかったり、施工の障害となる石垣の石が大量に出たりします。昔、氾濫の多かった河川敷の跡も支持層の高低差が大きい可能性があり、事前の詳細な調査が求められます。

しかし、最近では、地盤情報がデータベース化されているにもかかわらず、十分な事前調査もなく、流れ作業で基礎の設計をしているマンションを見かけます。今のところタワーマンションはそのような地盤には建設されていないようですが、いずれ建設用地が不足し、やむなく建てることになった場合は、入念な調査と慎重な設計が望まれます。

Studying Site History

Architects carefully study the historical background of the construction site in the case of large-scaled development project. There are ancient maps available for the Tokyo metropolitan area, particularly for the neighborhood of the Tokyo Station, and in fact, you can get some of them from the bookstores. Those maps contain essential historical information of the project site. Landfilled reservoirs and moats could cause construction problems like non-flat bearing stratum and numerous stones from stone walls. Also, old riverbeds that went through many floods may have rather big ups and downs and thorough assessment may be required.

Despite the fact that the grounds information is readily available in the database, some developers conduct foundation design routinely without thorough assessment. There seems no high-rise condo constructed on such grounds, but

Useful Information on Architecture

should that situation happen due to the land shortage, it is highly desirable to conduct thorough assessment and careful design.

溜池（現在の赤坂見附）付近の古地図（著者所蔵） Ancient Map Around Akasaka-Mitsuke

Chapter Z

エピローグ

Afterword

Chapter Z エピローグ

あとがき

建築に携わって、40年が過ぎようとしています。超高層建築に魅せられた学生時代は、工業化住宅の研究、就職後には、超高層ビルや半導体工場、ドーム、パビリオンの設計、営業、ビル管理、工事、そして、タワーマンションなど、様々な建築に関わってきました。しかし、最も身近な存在である住宅について、どのように計画され、どのようにつくられているかということについて、専門家といわれている人でさえ、建築主に対して十分に説明されているかというと、はなはだ疑問に感じることが多かったのも事実です。マンションに関しては、品確法など様々な法律があり、それに基づいて設計され工事完了後は検査済証などが交付されます。

しかし、完璧に近い書類が山積みされているにもかかわらず、現場では施工ミスが絶えません。解決の方向として、IT技術が導入されつつありますが、建築産業が一品生産労働集約型産業という性格上、効率化への道のりは遠いのが現状です。また、IT化が各社独自に進むことで、施工者が様々なソフトウェアを使いこなさなければならない状況になりつつあります。これについては、今後の国土交通省の役割に期待したいところです。

私自身がタワーマンションに暮らして14年近く、大規模修繕工事にも関わるなど様々な経験から、一生に一度かもしれない大きな買い物を、溢れる情報に惑わされることなく、自信を持って見極めてほしい、その一助となればと「タワーマンションの真実」として一冊にまとめてみることにしました。

出版に当たり、筆無精な私を叱咤激励して下さった建築画報社の櫻井社長に感謝の意を表したいと思います。

Afterword

Almost 40 years have passed since I started my career in architecture. Back in my school days, I was fascinated with ultra-high-rise architecture and studied industrialized housing. After graduation, I have been involved in various architectural projects of ultra-high-rise building, semiconductor plant, dome, and pavilion designs, as well as in sales, building maintenance and construction activities, and of course, in high-rise condo projects. During the course, I often wondered if the experts was doing their best to give sufficient explanation to the clients on how their houses are planned, designed and built. As far as the condos are concerned, they are designed and built conforming to various laws and regulations including the Housing Quality Assurance Act, and a certificate of completion will be issued once the construction is completed.

Even though there are piles of near perfect documents, they keep on making mistakes during construction. As a solution to this, IT is getting adopted, however, being one of the labor-intensive custom production industries, construction industry has a long way to go before making a reasonable progress in improving efficiency.

Also, as developers are taking different approaches in their IT adoption, constructors are forced to use different software depending on the developer. I would really hope the Ministry of Land, Infrastructure, Transport and Tourism would take some proper action about this.

I myself have been living in a high-rise condo for almost 14 years and had various experiences including an involvement in a large-scale repair. I prepared this book in hopes of helping people choose their once-in-a-lifetime purchase with confidence without getting confused with flood of information.

And at last but not least, I would like to express my sincere gratitude to Ms. Sakurai, the president of Kenchiku Gahou Inc. for her encouragements.

タワーマンションの真実
超高層建築のプロが教える
タワーマンションの見極め方

2016年10月28日 初版第一版発行
著：橋本友希
ブックデザイン：田中智康（グラムシ）

発行：建築画報社
160-0022 東京都新宿区
新宿2丁目14番6号 第一早川屋ビル
TEL. 03-3356-2568
www.kenchiku-gahou.com

定価：1,500円（税別）
印刷・製本：サンニチ印刷

乱丁・落丁本はお取り替えいたします
Printed in Japan 978-4-901772-97-6